Luck or Miracle

A World War II POW's Survival Story

By Reginald Bollich
As Told by James Bollich

Modern History Press

Ann Arbor, MI

Luck or Miracle: A World War II POW's Survival Story

ISBN 978-1-61599-777-0 paperback
ISBN 978-1-61599-778-7 hardcover
ISBN 978-1-61599-779-4 eBook

Modern History Press
5145 Pontiac Trail
Ann Arbor, MI 48105

www.ModernHistoryPress.com
info@ModernHistoryPress.com

Contents

Table of Figures

Foreword

In the course of the history of our Republic, many men have served valiantly to protect our rights, liberties, and freedoms. They have written a blank check, payable to the United States of America, for their service and in many cases their lives. It is vehemently believed that Providence has always guided this nation to become the most significant nation on the earth; allowing the people to be the masters of their destiny, rather than the government. Our Constitution, a unique document in history, established a form of government that, when challenged, was a rallying point for patriotic citizens to eagerly march to the sounds of guns to protect and preserve freedom for all mankind.

The unselfish actions of James Bollich are perfect examples of how dedication and love of country are manifested and have kept our country free. This interview is his personal narrative of how a humiliating defeat on the battlefield can turn your life upside down and create untenable situations that force one to overcome some of the most horrific situations imaginable (just to stay alive) and to realize that only through Providence can one survive.

The horrors of close combat are difficult to imagine unless one has been exposed to the fear, thirst, hunger, dirty filthy environment, fatigue, heat, cold, and other meteorological conditions that add to the misery of just staying alive. This is to say nothing of the high-speed metal flying through the air that adds to the personal concern on a continuing basis. Additionally, disease, infection, abdominal stress, insects, and an unethical determined enemy are there to create mental and physical anguish.

If this is not bad enough, when you are captured and held as a prisoner of war, a whole other dimension of complexity is added to the already stress-filled daily routine. Separation from family and the lack of ability to have routine worship of your Lord contributes to misery. The following discussion of James's experiences as a prisoner of war brings one close to understanding the distress, punishment, pain, and anxiety of suddenly being thrust into a horrific situation that lasted for over three and a half years. The amount of mental and physical toughness comes alive as his story unfolds.

America is eternally grateful for men like James who endured unimaginable pain and suffering, yet returned by the will of God to lead a productive and significant life. James, indeed, at one hundred and two, is still alert and productive and serves as an example of what each of us should strive to be. I am deeply honored to call him a friend. Let his story motivate you to be more thankful for the freedom we enjoy today because of these brave, dedicated patriots.

Major General Bob "Hawk" Hollingsworth,
USMC (Retired)

Preface

"Courage is not simply one of the virtues but the form of every virtue at the testing point."
- C.S. Lewis, *The Screwtape Letters*

The 102nd birthday of my cousin, James "Jim" Joseph Bollich, was celebrated on August 15, 2023, at his home in Lafayette, Louisiana. Jim is one of only two other Bataan Death March[1] survivors known to us who are alive today.[2]

As a World War II Prisoner of War (POW), Jim suffered and survived the worst atrocities that humans can perpetrate on one another, that is, crimes inflicted on him by the Imperial Japanese Army. But after he was freed from captivity and with the war over, he did not allow their brutal treatment to distract nor deter him from his interests and what he had to do. Upon returning home, he immediately resumed his college studies the war had interrupted, received two degrees in geology, married Celia Herndon (1924-2016), and completed post-graduate studies as a Fulbright scholar in Australia. Jim moved to Lafayette, Louisiana to earn a living as a geologist, raised his family, taught his two daughters the values of caring for wildlife, wrote fictional and non-fictional

---

[1] For Jim, it was an 8-day, 102-mile trek from Mariveles (09APR1942 @ 9:00AM) to Camp O'Donnell (~16-17APR1942). During the march, thousands of the captives were deprived of water, died of thirst, beaten, shot, bayoneted, and beheaded by their Japanese captors. Many more died in Camp O'Donnell of starvation and disease, mainly dysentery.

[2] Valdemar DeHerrera of Taos, NM and Irvin C. Scott of Richmond, VA

books, painted beautiful works of art on canvas, and crafted stained glass windows featuring fowl and fauna for his home. After retiring, he became a gardener of orchids and an avid bird watcher. In his backyard, he fed birds, raised raccoons, and nursed orphaned baby possums by feeding them with an eye dropper. Currently, Jim spends his time growing milk-weed and fostering caterpillars in meshed cages to help save Monarch butterflies from extinction. In the evening, he treats his furry nocturnal friends with leftovers, especially his most favored possum named "Gumbo."

In 1993 Jim published *The Bataan Death March: A Soldier's Story*, a book that narrates many of the events that are written in this book. The difference is the verbal treatment and details of his survival and suffering offered in this account, *Luck or Miracle*. This story is about *courage* and the will to live. It is told from the voice, coherent mind, and soul of a man, who at the age of 102, felt compelled to isolate and describe those times when his life was fleeting, when he specifically faced death from thirst, from explosives of aerial bombs, torpedoes, and a floating mine, from topside of a disabled ship in a violent sea storm, from being beaten, shot, or stabbed for no reason. Jim wanted to talk, so I listened, and captured his words on a voice recorder at his home in July 2023. I offer to you his words to read and pass on to others, especially our American youth, 'lest we forget'.

Reggie Bollich[3]
August 15, 2023

---

[3] Jim's 80 year old cousin who resides with his wife Dottie Compton in Lafayette LA.

Maps

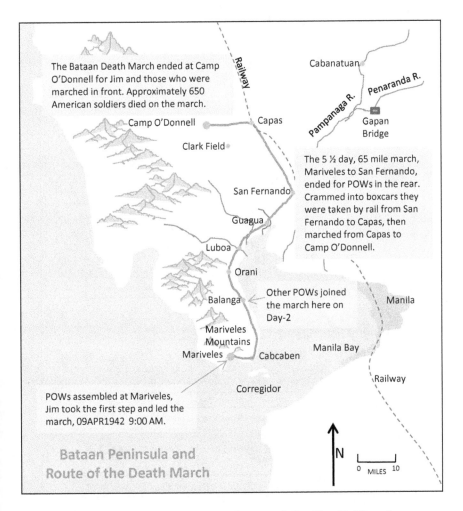

The Bataan Death March ended at Camp O'Donnell for Jim and those who were marched in front. Approximately 650 American soldiers died on the march.

The 5 ½ day, 65 mile march, Mariveles to San Fernando, ended for POWs in the rear. Crammed into boxcars they were taken by rail from San Fernando to Capas, then marched from Capas to Camp O'Donnell.

Other POWs joined the march here on Day-2

POWs assembled at Mariveles, Jim took the first step and led the march, 09APR1942 9:00 AM.

Bataan Peninsula and Route of the Death March

Map 1: Bataan Peninsula and the Route of the Death March

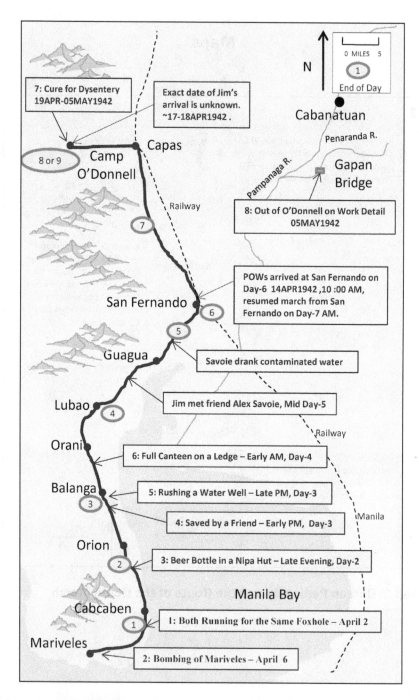

7: Cure for Dysentery
19APR-05MAY1942

Exact date of Jim's
arrival is unknown.
~17-18APR1942 .

Camp
O'Donnell

8 or 9

Capas

N

0 MILES 5

1

End of Day

Cabanatuan

Penaranda R.

Pampanaga R.

Gapan
Bridge

Railway

8: Out of O'Donnell on Work Detail
05MAY1942

7

San Fernando

6

POWs arrived at San Fernando on
Day-6 14APR1942 ,10 :00 AM,
resumed march from San
Fernando on Day-7 AM.

5

Guagua

Savoie drank contaminated water

Lubao

4

Jim met friend Alex Savoie, Mid Day-5

Orani

6: Full Canteen on a Ledge – Early AM, Day-4

Balanga

3

5: Rushing a Water Well – Late PM, Day-3

4: Saved by a Friend – Early PM, Day-3

Railway

Manila

Orion

2

3: Beer Bottle in a Nipa Hut – Late Evening, Day-2

Manila Bay

Cabcaben

1

I: Both Running for the Same Foxhole – April 2

Mariveles

2: Bombing of Mariveles – April 6

Map 2: Bataan Death March: 'Luck or Miracle' Events and Locations

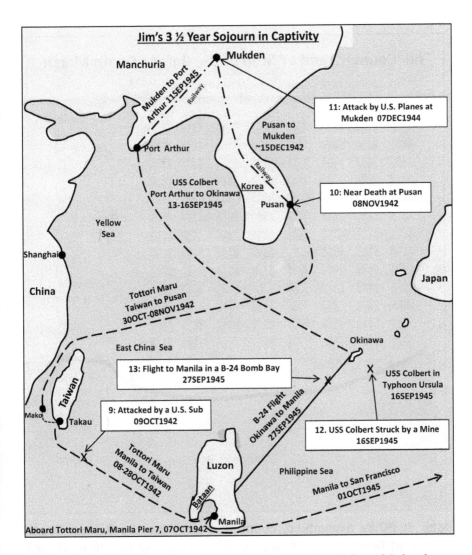

Map 3: Jim's 3-½ Year Journey and Sojourn in Captivity with Luck or Miracle Events and Locations

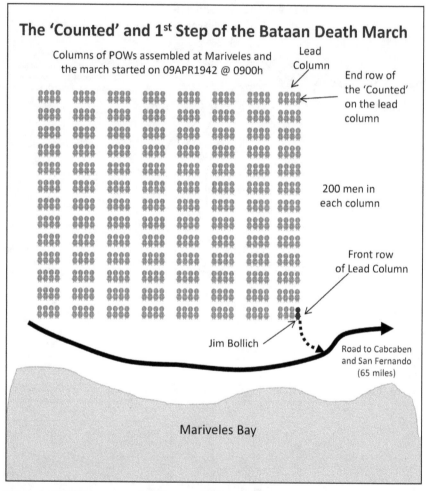

Map 4: POWs assembled, counted, and began the Bataan Death March at Mariveles on Thursday, 09APR1942 @ 0900h in Manila (Wednesday, 08APR1942 @ 2000h CT USA)

1   Was it Luck or a Miracle?

What made you decide to chronicle these thirteen compelling stories about your survival as a POW during World War II?

I've given talks before called "I Survived" to organizations such as the American Legion. I selected the bombing at Cabcaben Field[4] where I got the compass just before the start of the Bataan Death March, the B-29[5] bombing of Mukden Prison Camp[6] in Manchuria,[7] and riding out Typhoon Ursula[8] in the Philippine Sea aboard the USS Colbert[9] a few days after departing Manchuria and my release from captivity. I talked about only these three events, but it wasn't until we were having lunch here two or three weeks ago that

---

[4] An airfield located at the southern end of the Bataan Peninsula in the Philippines (Map 1).

[5] A U.S. made heavy bomber (a.k.a. Superfortress) used to bomb Japanese cities and drop atomic bombs on Hiroshima (06AUG1945) and Nagasaki (09AUG1945).

[6] A POW prison camp (a.k.a. Hoten) was located near the city of Mukden (a.k.a. Shenyang, China), where 1420 Allied POWs were held and 224 died in captivity (Top of Map 3). "Hoten Camp", 29JUN2023, https://en.wikipedia.org/wiki/Hoten_Camp

[7] The region of China and east Russia covers the entire northeast of China (Top of Map 3).

[8] A storm during September 1945 where six air transports were lost and 120 liberated U.S. POWs died (Map 3). (Cox, para 5) (history.navy.mil/about-us/leadership/director/directors-corner/h-grams/h-gram-057/h-057-1.html)

[9] A troop transport ship in service with the U.S. Navy (1945-46).

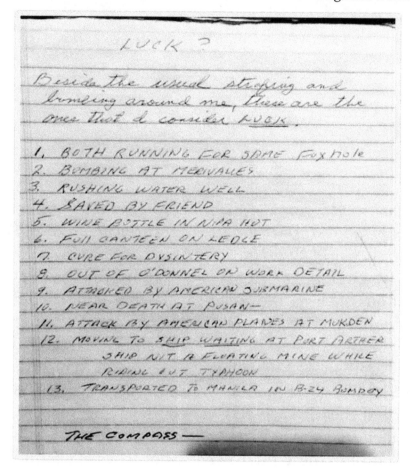

LUCK ?

Beside the usual strafing and bombing around me, these are the ones that I consider LUCK.

1. BOTH RUNNING FOR SAME Foxhole
2. BOMBING AT MEDIVALLES
3. RUSHING WATER WELL
4. SAVED BY FRIEND
5. WINE BOTTLE IN NIPA HUT
6. FULL CANTEEN ON LEDGE
7. CURE FOR DYSINTERY
8. OUT OF O'DONNEL ON WORK DETAIL
9. ATTACKED BY AMERICAN SUBMARINE
10. NEAR DEATH AT PUSAN —
11. ATTACK BY AMERICAN PLANES AT MUKDEN
12. MOVING TO SHIP WAITING AT PORT ARTHER
    SHIP NOT A FLOATING MINE WHILE
    RIDING OUT TYPHOON
13. TRANSPORTED TO MANILA IN B-24 BOMBER

THE COMPASS —

Photo 1: Jim's Handwritten Outline that started this book.

Dottie brought it up and got this started. That's when I decided to tell what I knew about the times I survived, those crucial moments when it could have gone the other way. There were more than three, and that's when I came up with thirteen and it was Dottie who decided that the title should be *Luck or Miracle* (Photo 1).

In several books I've read, authored by POWs, they wrote about their survival experiences and referred to them as miracles, so they do talk about miracles. In a few cases where guys were in situations similar to what

I refer to as *luck*, they mention that it was more than luck.

People often ask POWs, "Why did you survive when so many didn't?" I tell them that in my case there are three reasons: one is *prayer*, one is *luck*, and one is *my early lifestyle*.

As far as *prayer* goes, I answer, "Virtually everybody prayed in captivity." Then the next question would be asked, "If everybody prayed, why didn't everybody get back?" And I'd reply that those who believed, truly believed, and had a strong faith in the hereafter, then they figured why waste time in this so-called hell on earth, when you could give up and be in heaven within minutes, so many gave up with that thought. Now, I'm not sure that happens, but I think it is possible.

I prayed every night, and most of my prayers were for my family, that everything was fine. The only thing I prayed for regarding myself was that someday God would get me out of this mess, let me live for ten years or until I was thirty-five, and let me die in a clean bed. That's what I prayed for in captivity.

After arriving in Bataan, I never went to church because there was no opportunity, being overseas, then in a prison camp, and during a war, there were no chaplains. The Japanese prohibited the practice of religion, so there was no religion at all during the entire time of my captivity. My religion was nurtured solely as an individual because there was nobody to talk to or help me. That was it, as far as religion goes, I was on my own, strictly personal between me and God, period.

Growing up and to the time I left home to join up, my family was very devout. I went to a Catholic school, attended mass every Sunday, took communion, and went to confession. When I got back from the war, I wasn't interested in going to church. For many years as a POW, my religion was private, and it was my closeness to God that helped me get through hell on earth. I dare not change what got me through it. Today I have that same closeness of being alone with my thoughts, and that replaces going to a church. I do consider St. Lawrence Church in Mowata[10] to be my church and, until I couldn't, I went there to attend funerals, and where I took communion. Even today, I still must fall back to my surviving alone with God, that cannot change. It's how I survived and lived through hell on earth.

As far as my *luck* is concerned, it pertains to events that happened to me during my time fighting on Bataan, during the death march, in the camps where I was held captive, and on my way home at war's end. The events that I choose as *luck* are what had happened to me, where anyone of them could have caused major injury to me, or even death. But I survived, shaken by some, but essentially unharmed by all.

As far as *my early lifestyle*, I always liked being out-doors. As a boy and adolescent, I returned home from school, kick off my shoes, get into my stinky clothes, grab a rifle, and go hunting in the woods on the farm. Many times, and I probably should not say this because it is illegal now but wasn't back then, when the robins arrived in winter, I went out with my rifle, shot robins, cleaned them, put them on a stick, warmed them over a

---

[10] A rice farming community located in Acadia Parish LA, settled by German immigrants in the mid-late 19th century.

little fire, and ate them. I did that time after time after time. And I remember they were half cooked, the blood was kind of salty, didn't need any salt on that kind of meat.

In the Philippines, whenever I had time off, I did a similar thing. Now, I didn't get as many birds when I'd go out. The old World War I rifles we had were 30-30s, which were hardly any stronger than a 22. So, I used a 30-30 to shoot small birds and there was still a lot there to eat after shooting one. Once I managed to kill a little wild pig, and I brought it back to the camp to our cook who prepared it for me to share with others. Of course, I couldn't eat a whole pig. If there was no other game, I'd shoot a crow, whose meat is about as dark as the feathers and as tough as a boot. There's no doubt that I got a little bit of extra food that the other guys didn't get.

I'd like to tell two more pre-surrender hunting stories that still amuse me, about a couple of guys who became my friends after the war. The hunts happened when food was getting scarce, and after people found out that I hunted my food, especially after getting the first pig for them to eat. Others wanted to go with me on hunting expeditions but I liked hunting alone and did not want to take anyone with me.

Well, this guy insisted on going, so I decided to let him join me. We followed a streambed because the growth was too bushy along the banks to walk outside of the stream. We were walking on rocks and hopping from boulder to boulder in the stream. Coming to a very big tree that had fallen across the stream, we decided to climb on top of the log, and look around when suddenly two boars jumped out. I had my rifle poised to shoot and the guy with me shouts, "Don't shoot, don't shoot, don't shoot". And of course, they climbed up and got away. I think he was afraid that the noise of the rifle shot might alert the Japanese soldiers who were in the area. I never did ask him why, but I could have killed at least one of those boars and we'd have had a great feast that night. He was a good friend of mine, Summie B. Riley.[11] When I received my medal,[12] his family was there also to receive his medal because their father had passed away.

There was another guy, Myers. Johnny Myers[13] wanted to go with me but we did not go too far because it was getting late. We were at a very steep curve in the stream and were sitting on boulders while I was watching both sides of the stream. Some little pebbles started to fall near me from above. I looked up and said, "Snake!", and Myers was gone in a second. I could only see about that much of the snake because it was rough with vines and growth. The snake was a boa constrictor, about that round and I tried to find its head. I didn't know whether his head was that way or whether his head was that way (*motioning with his hands*). It was getting dark and I had to do something so I shot it, right through the belly. And I thought his head might turn my way, but then it just slid up into

---

[11] Riley, Summie B: Rank: Pvt,. POW - Bataan Death March and Mukden Camp survivor, Liberated: 15AUG1945, Unit: USAAC 16th Bomb Sqn/27th Bomb GP, From: Arkansas

[12] The Congressional Gold Medal, awarded by U.S. Congress, is the highest expression of national appreciation for distinguished achievement /contribution. 28APR2023, (https://en.wikipedia.org/wiki/Congressional_Gold_Medal)

[13] Myers, John S: Rank: Pvt, POW - Bataan Death March and Japan prison camp survivor, Unit: USAAC 16th Bomb Sqn/27th Bomb GP

the brush and took off. But the snake was really kind of past us and it was hunting like we were. It was waiting for something. There was no chance for it to fall on us but if it had been facing us that would have been different and I might not be here today telling this story. But snakes do not worry me, never did. Both Summie and Johnny got back home after the war and they died some time ago.

My last hunt on Bataan for something to eat came just before the surrender. As time went by, food to be hunted became even scarcer, and I went further and further into the foothills of the mountains to find something to eat. On this particular day, I was as far as I'd ever been in the foothills, and came across this huge fig tree that strangled another big tree. All that was left was the huge trunk of the strangled tree with fig vines climbing all around it. There was some fresh dirt around the base of the trees. I figured that an animal dug a hole, which meant I might find something to eat. But I noticed dirt higher up in the branches and thought, "Somebody did that," and maybe they were inside the hollow trunk. I had my pistol and rifle, put my rifle down, and crawled up to the top of the tree trunk, which was about fifteen to twenty feet high.

At the top, I slowly lifted my head over the edge, peered down the trunk, and could see that somebody had lived in there, or could still be in there. I backed out slowly, and on my way down I could clearly see our airfield. It was a perfect place to see our airfield that was way down below. We often wondered why the minute we put a plane out on the runway, the Japanese planes started coming to bomb us. It must have been their lookout point and the chances were good that somebody was still down inside that hollow trunk. I went back to the camp and planned to return with a grenade to drop down the trunk. But the surrender came and that was my last hunt.

2 Both Running for the Same Foxhole (01-02APR1942)

My job during the war was to operate a 50-caliber machine gun at an airstrip on the Bataan peninsula (Map 1). The machine guns were used to defend against any enemy aircraft. They were really home-made affairs mounted on tripods, placed in each of two pits, one pit on each side of the runway. The width of the runway was no more than five or six times the width of an airplane. The pits were circular, dug into the ground about two feet deep, and surrounded by sandbags.

The Japanese planes we encountered at the airstrip near the start of the war were dive bombers. They flew from over the mountain and were on top of us within seconds. By the time we were able to respond and shoot, they'd already passed. Their planes were accurate, dropping bombs directly on top of and in the center of the airstrip. After the dive bombers left the area, our engineers would drive graders onto the airstrip to cover up the bomb craters.

Early one morning, when I was being relieved of my shift and waiting for a ride back to the camp, which was located in the jungles, an engineer was operating a grader and filling potholes in the airstrip. Routinely, we saw Japanese heavy bombers flying overhead at high altitudes on the way to bomb Corregidor.[14] Up to this point the heavy bombers had never dropped bombs on our airstrip, only the smaller dive bombers that carried a single bomb attacked us.

But one day eight or nine heavy bombers turned around and I could tell they were headed back toward us. I could see shiny objects in the sky falling away from the planes and within a short time, black swooshing bombs came raining down on us. The engineer jumped off the grader and both of us started running for the foxholes that lined the airstrip. A single foxhole would have been large enough for both of us, but since he was ahead of me by a couple of strides, I decided to let him have the nearest one. So, I took the next one a bit further away.

Bombs were exploding all around but they were not all falling at the same time. They fell in a sequence and the noise of each explosion was heard in steps such as boom, then boom, and then another boom. Upon jumping into my foxhole, I raised my left arm to hold my helmet onto my head and my arm got peppered with fragments of shrapnel. Spontaneously, a bomb fell directly into the foxhole of the guy who was running in front of me. On the all-clear signal, I looked to see what happened to him but found nothing, except for a compass with the inscription "US Engineers Dept USA 1918." This is not the compass I found, but it is one exactly like it (Photo 2).

---

[14] An island located 21 miles south of Bataan Peninsula on Manila Bay in the Philippines (Map 1).

Photo 2: A compass similar to the one James Bollich used.

I kept the compass, hoping to identify the engineer who'd died and perhaps give the compass to his family after the war and tell them what had happened to him. But it was my last day in the field, and that's when all of us were pulled out, and I did not have time to identify this man. The shelling of the big guns on the front line was getting louder. As the Japanese were closing in on us, we abandoned camp and headed south. Everybody was being evacuated to the south.

Do you recall the name of the airstrip?

It goes by two names; Bataan Field or Cabcaben Field.

Was the airfield dirt or tarmac?

It was a dirt airstrip that was bulldozed and graded. It was a difficult job to maintain each side of the runway because of the huge boulders. Our plane, the P-40,[15] had no tricycle gear so a problem for pilots was

---

[15] A U.S.-made single-engine, single-seat fighter plan (a.k.a. Warhawk).

getting the nose down quickly for a clear view of the runway. The planes had to be pointed down the center of the runway with the nose down on takeoff to avoid those big boulders.

What was the length of a runway?

The runway started at the edge of the jungle, maybe a little longer than the length of a football field. Later on, we heard that we were going to get some bombers and planned to extend the runway to the water at the edge of Manila Bay. The bombers never arrived, of course.

Were you awarded the Purple Heart because of the shrapnel wounds you received from the bomb that hit the foxhole?

Right, but it may have been for something else. To receive the Purple Heart[16] a soldier or sailor has to have been bled by action from the enemy. After the war during my debriefing, I told our investigators about the beatings I endured and the countless times I was bloodied, so I don't know if it's both of those. I knew nothing about a Purple Heart before the debriefing, but after I was told to apply for one. I thought a Purple Heart might be a badge or something similar. I didn't know that soldiers received medals. Nobody received medals before the war, so awarding medals became a military practice during the war.

---

[16] The oldest U.S. military award medal.

Photo 3: General Eisenhower speaks to a paratrooper before the Normandy invasion. A typical musette bag is circled.

What happened to the engineer's compass that you kept?

The story about the compass begins at Mariveles[17] on the day when I was waiting to be relieved from my machine gun, and watching the guy patch holes that the Japanese dive bombers put in our airstrip. The story of the compass does not end until the day I was liberated at Mukden Prison Camp in Manchuria on my 24th birthday, August 15, 1945.

So, after the bombing at Mariveles, a truck came to pick me up, got to the camp, and I put the compass in my musette bag (Photo 3). Now, a musette bag consists

---

[17] A city located on the south shore of Bataan, the Philippines (Map 1).

of five parts: two bigger outer edges, but right in the middle, there are three small sections, small individual sections where things like a comb, toothbrush, or toothpaste can be inserted. I pushed the compass deep inside the middle of the three small sections. It was a perfect fit. At this time, I thought the war would go on, still not knowing that we were being surrendered.

When the surrender came and we started on the march, the first thing that the Japanese did was take everything we had. They pulled off our dog tags, and took our rings; some people had wallets so they took them. I had about fifty-dollars with me. I wore the Army Air Corps (ACC) coveralls and inside was an artificial belt made out of cloth so I cut a little hole, slipped my money in the belt, and threw my wallet away because it had nothing else in it. The Japanese took almost everything, and went through my musette bag, turning it over, shaking it, but the compass did not fall out, and oddly, I was able to keep my musette bag. So, I got by that deal.

Later on, I had no trouble getting the bag into the first camp, Camp O'Donnell. Still, later I carried it with me to the Gapan bridge detail without any trouble, no inspection, got on the hell-ship when we left Manila, still no inspection, and had it with me when I stayed in the hospital in Pusan with no inspection, got up to Mukden in the old prison camp, no inspection. But that's when I began to worry, at the old Mukden prison camp, because three guys escaped, and were later captured and executed.[18] I was afraid that the Japanese would search our barracks. My bag was at my bunk place in the camp, and I don't know if the Japanese ever went through it or not, but they could have checked it. But the compass wouldn't fall out unless someone knew it was down in that third section. Otherwise they wouldn't find it.

We left the old camp, moved to the new camp, and the Japanese figured they were not going to let any kind of contraband get into the new camp. We were being stripped naked. All we had on was Japanese clothes; a coat, shirt, trousers, socks, and shoes. We approached the guard one at a time, there were four or five different guards. As we approached, we'd hand the guard our shirt and he'd throw it behind him, we'd hand him our trousers, and he'd go through and throw the trousers behind him, we handed him our shoes and socks. Well, I was petrified. I had that compass, and I figured they were going to find it. I dug it out and attempted to put it in my mouth, but it had about an eight-inch string tied to it, and I couldn't get all of that in my mouth. I thought I was gone because if they found it, I'd be dead before the day was over.

This is what I did. Most of the guys started with a shirt, then their pants, and gave their shoes. Well, I went a little differently. First of all, I gave him my pants, and then my shoes. I had the compass hidden in my hand when I took off my shirt and handed it to the

---

[18] S/1C Ferdinand F. Meringolo: SA#233990, USS Canopus, NY; Sgt. Joe B. Chastain: SA# 270992 4th Marine Rgt, Co K, TX; Cpl Victor Pallioti: SA# 274301, 4th Marine Rgt, Co D, RI

"Mukden Time Line", Mansell.com, Roger Mansell, [n.d.] (mansell.com/pow_resources/camplists/china_hk/mukden/mukden_timeline.html)

guard using the same hand. But instead of throwing my shirt to him, I held it with my fingers with a compass hidden in my palm. So instead of throwing the shirt to the guard, I just reached over to him and he went through it and I threw it behind him. That was the closest, I'd say, that I came to being shot. So, after it was over with, I could not keep it on me anymore, this had gone too far.

The new barracks were built with different compartments, and the bunks were, like in all Japanese buildings, built about eight inches off from the floor, and there were little boards that extended from the top of the bunk down to the floor. I found one loose board, and I was able to pull it out, reached as far back as I could, put my compass on top of one of the supports that held the floor to the beds, and then put the board back. But I was a little suspicious. I asked myself, "Why would they leave something not nailed down?" But I had to get rid of it, didn't want it on me.

When the war ended, the first thing I went for was my compass. I pulled that little board off and I reached back there and the compass was gone. This is what I thought. Maybe one of the POWs saw me hide it and then stole it. I couldn't imagine the Japanese finding it because all hell would have broken loose. But years later, after the war at one of our ex-POW gatherings, when we were talking about the bombings at Mukden, this guy said to me, "I know what happened to your compass. When that bomb hit the barracks, the shock knocked the compass off the two-by-six and it was probably down on the ground next to where you put it. Many years later, the embassy in Mukden awarded my book as *Book of the Month*, and that's when they found out about my compass. They got in touch with me and said, "There's still a barracks there that the Chinese turned into a museum and your compass might still be there. What building were you in?" I told them it was the third building and found out later that the third barracks had been demolished. So, I never got the compass. My daughter, Melinda, found one just like it and I have it, but it's not the original.

When were you separated from the musette bag?

Left it at the end of the war in Mukden, didn't bring it back. It was a struggle during the march, starting with a blanket, mosquito net, and shoes on my feet. Along the march, the first thing thrown away were the blankets, no blankets. The next thing that went was the mosquito net, no mosquito nets. Pretty soon, people were just discarding weight. So, carrying that musette bag was a struggle, but I wasn't going to give it up on account of the compass. A lot of people gave up their shoes. I took off mine within the first days of the march; everybody had blisters, broken blisters, and bloody feet. Mine never did break at first because I took my shoes off and probably threw them away by the time I found that small can of rice in the mud, because I was barefooted, but I'm not positive of the exact time.

I was in the same clothes until I got to Pusan, in the same coveralls. The surrender was in April and it was November when we arrived in Pusan. I had the same clothes on, never been washed, never been off my body. Well once, the clothes did get washed when they took us off the ship at Formosa (Taiwan) to get hosed down.

I tried to clean my clothes, tried to wash them as much as I could with my feet on the ground because they made us strip naked and they hosed us off. But then they gave us Japanese uniforms and shoes at the hospital in Pusan.

Later on, I'm going to tell you about this book entitled *The Steadfast Line* that describes details about the 27th Bomb Group.[19] I've been in touch with the author for many years. She appeared at one of our reunions at Warner Robins Air Force Base in Georgia. She was a history professor at Florida State University, had an uncle who had died in the Philippines, and was from the 27th Bomb Group. So, she came to the reunion where at night we had a banquet. Well, on the first night, the poor woman was more or less by herself, nobody had approached her. Feeling sorry for her, I went to find out who she was and learned the story. I introduced her to everybody at the banquet and ever since then we've been good friends.

She has written the history of the 27th Bomb Group and her account is probably better than what they have in the War Department. The lady is from Tallahassee, Florida, and now she's retired. The last email I got from her was this week. She said that she remembered when I'd approached her at the reunion. She said she was shy back then but has kept in touch with a whole bunch of the guys. I asked her, "Do you know of anybody else who might be a survivor of the 27th?" She said, "For the last ten years, you are the only person that is left." That was this week. It was her uncle who was in the march

---

[19] Mary Cathrin May. *The Steadfast Line: The Story of the 27th Bombardment Group in WW II*, 2003

and so she just got interested in all of this. Her name is Mary Cathrin May.

3   Bombing of Mariveles
06APR1942

This happened only a few days after the bombing at the airstrip. After leaving Cabcaben Airstrip, I was taken back to camp along with many other soldiers. We were told of being relocated and to leave everything behind except essentials, such as a toothbrush, comb, etc. Emergency World War I rations, comprising crackers and bully beef, were handed out. There were ten crackers in a pack that was coated with paraffin and a small Pet Milk sized can containing bully beef. Everybody ate the emergency rations right off the bat. We were also offered extra shoes but I was satisfied with the shoes I had on my feet.

When we were ready to leave the camp, my friend, George Bramlett,[20] was missing. We searched and finally found him to be extremely ill, lying in some underbrush. He told us, "Leave me, I don't want to go, you go ahead." We couldn't leave him so we placed him in one of the trucks. It was not yet dark when we started down the road congested with people evacuating in great numbers to Mariveles. It seemed to me that we were, perhaps, dropping back and forming

---

[20] Bramlett, George R: Rank: T/5, Service #:14006598, MIA: 1AUG1942, Location: Philippines, Unit: USAAC 16th Bomb Sqn, 27th Bomb GP (Light), From: Claiborne Parish, LA (honorstates.org/profiles/50264/)

a new line to be protected by the big guns of Corregidor, but that turned out not to be the case.

The front lines were getting closer and by nightfall the bombs were loud and the cannon fire within hearing range. Upon arriving at Mariveles the next morning, we found an empty room with a bed near a building where others were assembling. We placed George in the bed, figuring this place was as good as any since he could barely move. The Japanese began strafing and bullets ricocheted through the building, so we decided it was not such a good place to be after all. Bruce Miller,[21] Alex Savoie,[22] and I moved George into some underbrush off to the side and away from the others but near a large foxhole. Meanwhile, Bruce found a tin can of coffee in one of the buildings so we built a fire to brew coffee. My camera was still in my knapsack so while we were waiting for the coffee to brew, I snapped a picture of the four of us.

I later buried the camera and the film nearby. It was found, and the photo was published, appearing in many books since that time.

There were numerous foxholes in the area and two officers stood nearby as we brewed our coffee. We could hear enemy heavy bombers coming, so the two officers jumped into foxholes and called out to us, "You'd better get into a foxhole." (Photo 4) We did, reluctantly, but later we were thankful because one

[21] Miller, Bruce: Rank: Pvt, POW - Bataan Death March and Japan prison camp survivor, Unit: USAAC 16th Bomb Sqn, 27th Bomb GP, From: St. Landry Parish, LA

[22] Savoie, Alex: Rank: T/5, Service:14014522, POW- Bataan Death March, Died: 13SEP1942, died under Japanese control, Unit: USAAC 16th Bomb Sqn, 27th Bomb GP, From: St Landry Parish, LA (honorstates.org/profiles/50730/)

Photo 4: Left-to-right, Miller, Savoie, Bollich, Bramlett in a foxhole on the day before General King surrendered (07APR1942).

bomb fell within ten feet of our position and we'd have been wiped out had we ignored their advice.

After the bombing ceased, we approached two other officers who were in a jeep. On the rear of the jeep was mounted a visible white (truce) flag. I asked if they could help George so they helped me place him in the jeep. "Where are you guys going?" I asked. They replied, "Going to see if we can meet up with the Japanese." I cannot remember exactly why, but I ended up in the jeep with them. Instead of going around the bay side of the road to meet the Japanese, the officers drove on the Pacific side, but we weren't gone very long. A fighter plane dived on us and one of the officers said, "Stay where you are." The plane did not shoot

Photo 5: General Edward King discussing terms of surrender with a Japanese officer. From left, General King, Colonel Everett Williams, Major Wade Cothran, and Major Achille Tisdelle.

and just flew off. The officer who was driving decided to turn around and we went back to where everybody else was. That's where we waited for the Japanese and it was also the last time I saw George Bramlett.

On April 8, General King[23] (Photo 5) surrendered, the Japanese counted us, and on April 9 at nine o'clock in the morning the march started, which is very interesting because of where I was positioned as the march began. They lined us up in columns of two-hundred men each; four men in a row and about fifty rows in a column. There were many columns all lined up perpendicular to the road that ran parallel along the shoreline of

---

[23] Major General Edward P. King led the defense of the Bataan Peninsula against the Japanese invasion. The official recording of King's surrender is 09APR1942. Jim's POW journal records the surrender date as 08APR1942, the date used in this book to mark the surrender and post-surrender events until Jim entered Camp O'Donnell.

Mariveles Bay.[24] I was positioned on the rightmost end of the first row of the lead column (Map 4).

Two Japanese guards approached, looked at me, and did this *(hand sign to sit down)* while speaking in Japanese. I asked the guy next to me, "What does he want?" Somebody replied, "He wants you to sit down." So, I sat down and immediately received a crack across the head with a rifle butt. So, I jumped right back up, knowing that was not what he meant. The guard pushed me toward the road, wanting me to start walking, and I was the first one to take the first step of the Bataan Death March (Photo 6). Everybody started walking and within minutes Japanese troops swarmed around us and began stealing what little we had. They beat us unmercifully from the beginning of the march, which wound up and around into the hills, three or four miles from Mariveles.

Was George Bramlett with you in that foxhole of four men?

Yes, he was with us at the end when we took the photo. He was one of the four and very sick at that point. He didn't make it. After the war I saw that he was listed as missing-in-action.

After the war, the photo was spotted by Bruce Miller, who was with me when the picture was taken. He asked if I had seen the photo, but I had not. Later, I ran across it, published in a book, and I recognized it right away. The photo seems to have appeared in the U.S.

---

[24] U.S. Mariveles Naval Section Base for the U.S. fleet was the site of the surrender. The Bataan Death March began at the airfield runway.
(military-history.fandom.com/wiki/Mariveles_Naval_Section_Base)

Photo 6: Thousands of POWs marched from Mariveles to Camp O'Donnell. Jim, positioned in the first row of the lead column, took the first step to start the march (09APR1942).

before the war ended. I hid my camera loaded with film in a large pile of roof slates so the Japanese would not find it. I thought I'd eventually return to get the camera. After we left, the Filipinos may have searched the area and found the camera because the people who published it were the AP of the Philippines. So apparently it got to the Associated Press of the Philippines. They are the ones who released the photo to the media and it appeared in the States before the war ended.

Where did you buy your camera?

In Hawaii at a PX and had it with me when the war broke out. I also bought the last eight rolls of 35-mm film at the PX in Manila. One roll was in the camera so there were seven undeveloped rolls. When we left our camp in the jungles, I placed the undeveloped rolls in an empty wooden ammunition box, placed the box in a foxhole, covered the box with dirt, and took off. Those rolls of film are probably still there. After the war I was told, if I ever wanted to return to Bataan, I could go back and look for something, stuff like that, but I never wanted to go back.

In the days before the surrender by General King when things were seemingly desperate with the Japanese approaching, were you and the troops around you nervous or frightened?

I was never afraid of the Japanese, now that's my problem. But we had guys, I hate to say this, but when the war broke out we had guys who hid. We had our first sergeant; you'd swear that he could win the war by himself. He gave orders, but when the war broke out, he wouldn't even leave our camp up in the jungles. So, they broke him, replaced him right off the bat, and put another younger guy who was good. We had guys that would never leave in the morning. When everybody else took off to do their job, they'd go in the bushes and stay there all day long. Nothing could be done about it, or at least, nobody did anything about it.

Some of them just didn't have the nerves. It took a little while to get used to it that first day. I thought every bomb dropped and every bullet shot was coming at me, but here's what changed my mind. We were already on Bataan and I was on our little airstrip. Some ants were running around so I grabbed some little pebbles and tried to hit the ants but I never hit a single ant. That convinced me those bombs are the same way, if I can't hit an ant with a rock then bombs dropped from ten-thousand feet will not get me either, no. Although they came close, they didn't get me.

The minute we got to Bataan, we selected a place to camp away from the airstrip way up and under all the big jungle trees. And once we got up there, some men wouldn't leave. Well, they left after we were surrendered. Right before the surrender, let me tell you what else happened to that first sergeant who could win the war. I heard him say, "I'll survive, they're going to take us to a camp, they're going to feed us and clothe us, and all we have to do is waiting until the war ends." He survived the march, apparently, but was dead within six to seven weeks. He thought he had it figured out. But his replacement was good, I mean, a brave younger guy.

4   Beer Bottle in a Nipa Hut
10APR1942

Late one night, (April 10), I was able to get some rest when it was dark even with Japanese guards on each side of us. Ahead, I could see a small nipa hut (Photo 7) so I was able to jump out of the line without being seen; sneak into the shack, and get a little bit of rest. There was another guy already in the shack who had the same idea, so we stayed only long enough for a brief rest. There was a bunch of empty beer bottles in the shack so

Photo 7: This contemporary nipa hut is located near the Sarnelli House orphanage at Don Wai in northeast Thailand.

we each grabbed a bottle and got back in the line. At least I had something to carry water.

Before long, we came to Japanese soldiers camped near one of the water wells, kind of back in the woods. We were able to sneak out, fill our beer bottles with water, and get back in line. The next morning (April 11), I carried the bottle of water by holding it with my arm, hidden beneath my Air Corps coveralls. Around mid-morning, the guy who was with me in the shack broke out his bottle of water and started drinking. The guards saw him and beat the devil out of him with the bottle and other objects. That's when I figured, "Oh, I better get rid of this," so I let the bottle slip down inside the leg of my trousers. Afterwards, I thought dropping the bottle wasn't a good idea because there was water left in the bottle. Perhaps, behind me, a POW would find it, think it was a miracle, or worse, get beaten for drinking from it. But I dropped it, got rid of it.

So, by the end of the third day (April 11) I was out of water again. We marched all day until sundown. That evening, there was a change of Japanese guards so the soldiers guarding us during the first three days of the march were apparently being replaced with other Japanese soldiers who seemed less hostile. I figured that the guards during the first three days had been fighting in battles so they took their revenge on us. I later learned that the POWs who were marching in the rear were beaten and treated with much more brutality than those of us in the front. The weaker ones who lagged were beaten, shot, or stabbed to death. They killed those who couldn't keep up the pace.

5   Saved by a Friend
                         11APR1942

After the war, my friend, Herbert Lanclos,[25] whom we called Herbie, was telling people how he had saved my life. I could not imagine how this could be. One day he was visiting when my son-in-law, Stephen, was also visiting me in Lafayette. So, Stephen asks Herbie, "How did you save Jim's life?" That's when he told his story that I will repeat here.

All during the march, I was mostly marching with no one I knew. But one night (April 11), I happened to run into a good friend, Herbert Lanclos from Lafayette, who was in my outfit. It was either the second or third night of the march, and I was straggling. A Japanese guard didn't like how fast I was moving so he started pushing on me and I pushed back. The guard pushed on me again and I pushed back again. I wasn't about to be pushed around until two Japanese guards came forward and pointed their bayonets at my belly. That's when Herbie stepped in, pulled me back, and cautioned me to not push back any further. I was desperate and didn't care what happened to me. I wouldn't let a Japanese push me around. Well, that was a mistake.

---

[25] Lanclos, Herbert: Rank: Pvt, POW - Bataan Death March and Japan prison camp survivor, Unit: USAAC 16th Bomb Sqn, 27th Bomb GP, From: Lafayette Parish, LA

Herbie and I were in the same camp in Mukden, at the same hospital in San Antonio, with me on the same train going home and that's when I found out my two brothers had died in Europe. After Herbie returned to his home in Lafayette, he had a lot of trouble, having tried to commit suicide for a while. Eventually, he got a job as a switchman on the railroad, and died quite some time back.

Did you receive any communication from the States?

None at all during the war, it was four and a half years without a word. The good thing about it, the day before Bataan fell all the airplanes were getting ready to leave. One pilot came up to me and said, "I'm taking off, you want to write a note, give me a note and I can send it home." He had a pad so I wrote the note and took him up on his offer. Not knowing what was in store for me in the days ahead, I wrote on his pad, "I'm fine, don't worry about me," and he sent that message to my home. But the note was postmarked from the island of Cebu,[26] so when Bataan fell, my family thought I was not involved, that I was safe on Cebu Island. It was later that my parents began to worry when they received word that I was declared missing-in-action. A year and a half elapsed before the army listed me as a POW, so for my poor parents I was missing-in-action up to that point.

[26] A province of the Philippines located in the center of the archipelago.

6 Rushing a Water Well
11APR1942

On the first day (April 9), we marched all day without food, water, or rest. We did stop the first night and the Japanese surrounded us with machine guns. They didn't give us water or food, but at least we were getting a rest. The next morning, at the crack of dawn (April 10), they got us up and resumed marching. It was probably about midday that we became desperate for water. We marched past several artesian wells that were within twenty or twenty-five feet away, but they marched us past the wells and wouldn't give us water. It looked like they were trying to kill us and I believe that was their intention.

This happened late on the third day (April 11) of the march. It was getting dark, I was desperate, and decided to rush to the next water well we came to. I did not care; I was going to get water because I could not march further without it. I wasn't the only one with that same idea, because several of us headed for it when we came to the next well. I managed to get there before the others and drink a couple of good mouthfuls. Mud was all around the well and I was kind of stooping because the Japanese were shooting, and killing people at the well. Having removed my shoes much earlier, my feet had blistered and became more sensitive, which was maybe a blessing. I stepped on something in the mud and picked it up. Later, I peeled off muddy banana leaves, and found a small can of warm rice, like one of those small Pet Milk deals. I couldn't believe it, clean rice wrapped in banana leaves. So, I managed to get a drink without being shot and scurried back in line on the road with something to eat. Continuing, we marched during the night. You might presume this to be terrible, but it was one of the best things about the march that happened to me. The climate at night was cooler.

7   Full Canteen on a Ledge
12APR1942

Then I did get water once again. We went through this little barrio. I don't remember the name, but we were marching past and close to some buildings. It was early in the morning (April 12) when I noticed ahead that there was a stucco building with a ledge, a window ledge. I could see a canteen sitting on top of the ledge, probably placed there by a Filipino who wanted at least one of us to have water. After getting close enough, I grabbed it and couldn't believe it was full of water. I kept that canteen from then on. We reached a point as we approached San Fernando where we were away from the real bad Japanese troops, because I remember not caring whether they saw me drink.

Were you able to get at least a drink of water each day?

Oh no, let's see, no water the first two days until the second night at the nipa hut, then the third day at the well, then again from the canteen on the ledge, which I kept throughout my captivity. When we arrived in San Fernando (April 14), people were able to get water. They gave us a small amount of rice and water, so I must have filled my canteen. I just can't remember if I did or did not. But the fifth day (April 13) was very hot and I ran out of water early. The day was really a blank but I do remember two things. First, I met Alex Savoie sometime during the day. We walked together in the heat, didn't say much to each other, became weary, and desperate for water. Second, we walked all night long, and during the night, off the side of the road, I spotted a pond. Without being seen, we sneaked to the edge but I could smell a foul odor, it was bad water. Looking closely, I noticed decomposed bodies in it so I backed away and did not drink. But Alex did drink and he died from dysentery within weeks after we reached Camp O'Donnell.[27]

How many days from the time that you were captured and placed in front of the line until the time you reached San Fernando?[28]

Five and a half days from Mariveles to San Fernando. We started (April 9) at about nine or ten o 'clock and arrived at San Fernando at nine or ten on the sixth day (April 14). Those of us who marched in front walked the entire distance to Camp O'Donnell, the whole way (Map 2). I do not recall exactly how long it took us to arrive. In San Fernando, however, most of those in the rear were crammed in boxcars on a train for the last thirty miles. We were met by General King when we arrived at the gate of Camp O'Donnell.[29]

Of all the books that I've read, nobody mentions anything about General King giving us a speech. He and the Japanese camp commander[30] met us and

---

[27] A U.S. military reservation became the destination for POWs on the march. (Map 1).

[28] A city located 65 miles north of Mariveles where POWs marched to its train station.

[29] The exact date of General King's message is unknown, otherwise, the date Jim entered Camp O'Donnell might be known. After leaving San Fernando, Jim and 200+ POWs walked to Camp O'Donnell and entered late one afternoon (~16-17APR1942).

[30] Captain Yoshio Tsuneyoshi, known for his 'welcome speech' at Camp O'Donnell, was tried by the U.S. Eighth Army military commission in Yokohama after the war,

General King was the first one to speak. He said, "Don't feel bad. You're not the one who surrendered." He continued, "I'm the one that surrendered you. When we get back to the States, I'll take full responsibility for it." Then, of course, the Japanese camp commander got up and laid down the rules of the law[31], that if we broke the law we'd be shot and all that kind of stuff. Then we entered the camp.

What went through your mind during the march when you were dying of thirst?

I didn't know how long the march would last. On the first day I thought, "It has to end today," and then the next day, "How much longer, certainly it will be over by the end of the day." Then the next morning came, I got up, started walking and I'd think, "Certainly, we'll get there today and it will be over," but the evening came and I'd say to myself, "Probably tomorrow. We'll arrive at wherever they are taking us," but tomorrow came and it was the same. No water in the heat and just kept walking. The fourth day came, "Gosh, surely today is the day when we're going to stop." Fifth day, same thing, I'd think about water, but not knowing when it's going to end is almost as bad as not having water. And then we arrived at last. There was water at Camp O'Donnell, but it came out of only one spigot available for all of us to drink. People lined up day and

---

was found guilty, and sentenced to life imprisonment at hard labor (08OCT1947). (Browne, "USA vs Toshio")

(mansell.com/pow_resources/camplists/philippines/Cabanatuan/IMTFE_Case230_TS UNEYOSHI_Cabanatuan.pdf)

[31] (McManus, para 4)

night to get water out of one spigot, and many people had no way of holding the water. I had my canteen.

You mentioned some time ago that the Australians and British, mainly the Australians who were on this march, were treated differently, and allowed to keep their equipment and uniforms.

No British or Australians were on the march. We ran into some of them later when they were placed in our camp in Mukden. That's when we found out that they were in their uniforms and didn't get the same treatment as we did. The British were captured in Singapore. I have a list of all the POWs who were held in Mukden. Later, toward the end of the war, the high-ranking people were brought to our camp. We had the governor of Singapore. The only guy who wasn't with us was General Wainwright,[32] who was kept separately in Manchuria about a hundred miles north of Mukden.

Were Filipinos treated even worse than you were on the march?

We didn't march with the Filipinos. I have no idea where they were, behind us or in front of us, or what. But here's the deal. They were in a separate part of Camp O'Donnell, dying at the rate of four hundred a day while Americans were dying at a rate of forty per day.[33] Although there were many more Filipino POWs, we couldn't understand why they were dying so much faster than we were. The Japanese turned all of the

---

[32] General Jonathon Wainwright surrendered on Corregidor (06MAY1942) and held captive for 3 years in the Sian Prison Camp northeast of Mukden.

[33] An estimated 26,000 Filipinos and 1,500 Americans died in Camp O'Donnell in the weeks following the march. (Norman, para 2)

(britannica.com/event/Bataan-Death-March. Accessed 22SEP2023)

Filipino prisoners loose, so Filipinos were captive for only about a month. The rate at which they were dying was perhaps the reason the Japanese decided to let them go.

8   Cure for Dysentery
19APR-05MAY1942

It wasn't long after I arrived at Camp O'Donnell, within the first two weeks perhaps, that I came down with diarrhea or dysentery. Not sure which disease I had, but I am almost certain it was caused by the water I was drinking since I had almost no food to eat. Now I have no idea where I got the information about a small four feet high bush[34] that grew in the area and was said to cure dysentery. Anyway, these little bushes were growing inside of the prison yard. I filled both of my pockets, stuffing them full with leaves which I ate, and within a couple of days, I was well. But then the word had gotten around that the leaves were good for dysentery and within days the little bushes were stripped.

Anyone who caught dysentery after that died. Almost no one recovered from dysentery, one of the most horrible ways in the world to die. People lasted two to four weeks and then died in filth. The place was covered with flies so thick in places that bunches of them would fall off the edge of the barracks where we

---

[34] Tsang Gubat, an herbal shrub that grows in the Philippines, is used to relieve dysentery and diarrhea. Jim ingested the leaves at the onset of dysentery and claims the plant saved his life.

"Tsaang Gubat or Wild Tea.", philippineherbalmedicine.org, Philippine Herbal Medicine, 2005-2022, (philippineherbalmedicine.org/tsaang_gubat.htm)

were staying. It was unbelievable, poor guys naked next to and around open latrines covered with flies and no way to keep clean. I had a board that served as a plate for the food I was given. If a fly landed on my board of food, I threw the food away because every fly carried disease.

Did you encounter any other diseases or illnesses at Camp O'Donnell?

Aside from dysentery, which was the ninety-five percent killer of all diseases, people became ill from various others, especially cerebral malaria, which is deadly. I did not come down with other diseases until reaching Cabanatuan.

However, about five weeks after the dysentery episode at Camp O'Donnell, I had severe sunstroke. My job assignment was digging graves for the thirty to forty or so, of the total who died each day. The graves being dug were four feet wide, eight feet length, and about four feet deep. One day we were only about halfway through digging this large grave when I got very dizzy, felt faint, and was about to pass out. I did not have a hat and no drinking water. I do not know why, but on that day I had left my canteen in my bunk, which was a loft. Undoubtedly, I was suffering from sunstroke and felt like I was going to collapse.

So, I crawled out of the hole and started walking toward the Japanese guard who was there with us, but before I could reach him my eyesight gave out. I could not see and do not remember much after that except one of the guys digging with us took me back to the camp and put me in my loft at the barracks, really a shack, where we slept. I was having severe chills and burning up with fever, alternating between chills and burning up. About eight hours later, in the evening, my vision slowly returned and the fever and chills diminished. I do not remember how long it took me to recover but, of course, I finally did.

9   Out of O'Donnell on Work Detail
05MAY1942

One miracle for me was to be put on the Gapan[35] bridge work detail that left Camp O'Donnell. On this project we actually slept in sometime, on the floor of the schoolhouse. Our job was to rebuild a big bridge that had been blown up during the war. The bridge was to be rebuilt over a river using heavy timbers. We were in a clean place near the river so we had all the water we needed. I do not remember exactly how many people were on that detail, perhaps thirty-five, but some of them died.[36] The good thing about it, we buried them in individual graves. When the detail work ended, they transported us to Cabanatuan[37] because Camp O'Donnell was closed due to the rampant disease. Cabanatuan eventually turned out to be as bad as Camp O'Donnell.

Did you go back to Camp O'Donnell again?
No, they'd already closed it.

Did you bury a lot of people at Camp O'Donnell?
I buried a lot of people but never kept a tally. I don't remember where the greater burial detail was; at Camp

---

[35] A city 40 miles northwest of San Fernando and 21 miles south of Cabanatuan in Nueva Ecija, Philippines (Map 1).
[36] (Moody. 188)
[37] A city in Nueva Ecija, Philippines was location of a major WWII POW prison camp (Map 1).

O'Donnell or Cabanatuan. I've thought about that a lot, still think about it, and have never forgotten the misery of those who suffered and died. In my thoughts about them I often ask, "If there is a God, why did He allow them to suffer so much?" Well, it happens. And I cannot explain why I have been so lucky to have escaped death so often. Since the war ended, and to this day, I do not get emotional about death, and nor do I look at a dead person laid in a coffin.

How long were you at Camp O'Donnell?

About a month, until I left to go on the Gapan bridge detail. I recall the meals at Camp O'Donnell. Besides rice, we had boiled sweet potato vines and boiled carrot tops, which nobody could eat because they were too bitter. Later on, instead of just dried rice, they started making rice soup. We hadn't seen any dishes so I ate off a board that served as a plate. There were piles of bamboo everywhere at Camp O'Donnell, leftover bamboo sections as big as your leg. Later, I was able to find a nice piece of bamboo and made the perfect cup for my meals. That's when I got rid of the board.

What were the diseases you mentioned earlier when you became ill at Cabanatuan?

Once reaching Cabanatuan from Gapan, I came down with hepatitis and scurvy at almost the same time. The hepatitis caused me to lose my appetite completely, not being able to eat the dried rice, sweet potato vine, or carrot tops we were being fed. Simultaneously with hepatitis, I had a case of scurvy. It begins in the scrotum and I hate the word jock-itch, but that's what it feels like. The scrotum gets sore and scaly. We were experiencing this disease because we weren't eating anything that contained vitamin C.

After hepatitis and scurvy, the symptoms of beriberi set in. There are two types of beriberi. One is known as the dry type and the other is the wet type. The dry type affects the hands or feet from which there is suffering from severe pain. As far as I know, the dry type is not fatal. With the wet type, there is no pain but it is a lot more dangerous. The wet type starts in the ankles and swelling continues into the arms and legs. I had the wet type but the swelling did not reach my stomach. When it reaches the stomach, then apparently it is deadly.

One day, while eating dried rice I came into contact with one of the guys who sat next to me, we were eating together. He turned to me and asked, "Do you want the rest of this rice? I cannot eat anymore. " So I took it, ate it, and he died a day or so later from diphtheria. My imagination got the best of me. Man, I sweated for a week or two, but nothing happened. We knew diphtheria was highly contagious and it was being spread around the camp, but I was able to avoid that one.

What is dried rice?

Good rice is hard to cook. We cooked rice in large kettles with a wooden cover, so the steam was never sealed inside the kettle to cook properly. The kettles were filled with hot water and then kept over a fire. The rice was not evenly cooked, carbon would form around the edges from burnt rice and the entire kettle of rice tasted like it was burned. The burnt rice from the edges was eaten by people who had dysentery, thinking that might help, but it didn't, of course. The rest of the rice was half-cooked and that's where the name dried rice comes from. We'd chew it. It had a little softness on the outside, but it was mostly hard on the inside. It depended on where the rice was taken from the kettle, some overcooked and scorched, some undercooked or semi-cooked, and if you were lucky to get a spoonful from the center it might be properly cooked rice.

What happened after Cabanatuan?

After staying there, I was selected to go with a group that was leaving the Philippines. I have no idea how I was selected. I believe we were the first group to leave though. We went to Manila[38] and spent the first night in a warehouse where a large number of sacks containing dried fish were stored. The Filipinos had their sacks woven out of rice straw. I was able to wiggle my hand through one of the sacks and found these little tiny fish[39] that were dried and cured with salt. So, I filled my pockets with dried fish and lived on that until we were taken off the ship at Taiwan when we were hosed off. That's all I ate while on that hell-ship and I had a canteen full of water. I still had that canteen.

---

[38] The largest city and capitol of the Philippines (Map 1).
[39] Dilis, a small anchovy-type of fish, is popular in the Philippines. "Dilis.",AboutFilipinoFood.com, 28NOV2008, (aboutfilipinofood.com/dilis/)

10   Attacked by U.S. Submarine
09OCT1942 at 8:00 AM

Photo 8: Tottori Maru was a Japanese Imperial Navy Hell-ship. Jim was in the forward hold.

We were taken aboard this Japanese hell ship Tottori Maru (Photo 8) and I noticed as we boarded that it had some fake cannons mounted. The fake cannons were logs that were made to look like they were real. There were two thousand of us. The ship had two holds;[40] one in front and they packed about five-hundred of us in the front and about fifteen-hundred in the back. I was in the first hold and I remember going all the way to the back. I think the hell-ship was one of the worst incidents I went through during the war, as far as horrible. Well, I guess the most horrible was watching people die at Camp O'Donnell of dysentery.

At night, all we could do was sit and stand. We had no room for anything else. Unfortunately, some of the

---

[40] Cargo chambers where the POWs were held.

guys had dysentery and at night, the Japanese closed the hatch, and wouldn't let anybody out. The toilet facilities were outside the topside, hanging off the side of the ship. They'd only let two guys out at a time, but at night they closed the hold. No lights, dark, blackish pitch and all night long there was moaning and screaming. The guys with dysentery were not only soiling themselves but also the people around them. And gosh, it was miserable.

It was the second day out when we felt the ship make a strong curve to the right. You could hear the Japanese on the topside screaming, running around, really excited about something, and then explosions rocked the ship. My first reaction was, I thought, that we'd run across the American Navy and they were firing shells at us. I was hoping they'd sink us, thinking I might be able to get off the ship and be rescued, but it wasn't that at all.

The explosions were depth charges that the Japanese were rolling off the ship because we were attacked by an American submarine[41] (Photo 9). The skipper saw two torpedoes head at us and was able to turn the ship to the right. Supposedly the torpedoes missed by about fifty feet. The good thing was that America's early torpedoes weren't very accurate and it wasn't until later on that they had torpedoes that worked. So, if this had been later on, then we'd have been hit. This is one of the most excitable times I had. I was sure that the submarine was going to continue following us. I thought, "Tonight it's going to get right up to us and

---

[41] USS Spearfish (SS-190) was a U.S. Navy submarine that scouted the South China Sea between Manila and Taiwan (08SEP1942 and 11NOV1942).

it's going to blow us out of the water" and I waited for the blast all night long. Then I'd think, "If they blow a hole in the ship tonight I might be able to escape." It's the only time I worried that I'd die, but it didn't come. I don't know why that sub gave up. The skipper gave up. I thought, "I'd have followed that ship and sunk it." After that, I guess, the Japanese skippers wanted a convoy because of the problems they were having with getting torpedoed.

Photo 9: USS Spearfish under Lieutenant Commander James Dempsey. The sub fired torpedoes at the Tottori Maru (09OCT1942 @ 0800h).

11   Near Death at Pusan
08NOV1942

It got so bad inside the ship they stopped at Taiwan, took everybody off the ship, hosed us down on the dock with fire hoses and that gave us a chance to wash off the clothes that we were still in from the time of the surrender. They washed out the interior of the ship because it was infested with diarrhea and with the dead who had died from dysentery. So, they cleaned out the ship. It was November and it was cold when they put us back on the ship. We were soaking wet, our clothes were wet, and everything inside the ship was wet. Everyone was cold, wet, and miserable. I remember an officer telling me to be careful and try not to catch a cold. But unfortunately, I did.

We started sailing north and the next day my chest began to hurt on one side, and before long there was a pain on the other side. That's when I wound up with pneumonia. By the time we landed at Pusan,[42] I could hardly breathe, so weak, couldn't move, flat on the metal floor of the ship in the hull. I was on the verge of death, no doubt about it.

After we landed, the guys, who were able, crawled out of the hold onto a metal ladder and left. But there were a whole bunch of guys still inside as bad off as me

---

[42] A port located on the southeast tip of the South Korea coast, a.k.a. Busan. (Map 3)

and a lot of dead people in there, too. When it was my turn to be hauled out, they grabbed my feet and legs and handed me up to the Japanese at the hatch who grabbed me by both of my arms. I don't know how I didn't pass out. They took me on shore and literally threw me in the back of a truck and probably on top of some dead people.

In Pusan, I woke up inside of barracks, which was a stable, being used as a hospital room. I do not know how, but my musette bag and canteen were still with me. A Korean doctor and his assistant came, checked me out, and said I had double pneumonia. And that's when he started giving me that medicine, a white powder wrapped up in what looked like cigarette paper. If that ship had not landed when it did, another day and I'd have been one of the dead for sure.

I was in the hospital for four or five weeks with others who were also weak and sick. Eventually, we reached the point where we were able to get up and start walking around. That's when we were told we were well enough to leave Pusan. But some died in the hospital, were taken out, cremated, and their remains brought back in small jars. So, we survivors were given new clothes, finally getting rid of the old clothes we still had on. The new clothes comprised a summer Japanese uniform with shoes and socks. Then we left Pusan, each given a few jars of cremated remains to carry and be buried when we got to the next prison camp in Mukden, Manchuria.

It was winter, sometime between late November and Christmas. There was a lot of snow on the ground in Pusan when they put us on a train bound for Mukden.

The train stopped several miles outside of Mukden before reaching the central railway station downtown, and they took us off the train. The countryside was covered with snow, bitterly cold, and got to the point where I could hardly feel my feet from the cold. Eventually, a truck came, picked us up, and brought us to the camp where other POWs were housed.

When we got there, I went into one of the barracks and someone said, "Your nose is frozen. I'm going to go out and get some snow." Now I didn't know how that would work, but then somebody else said, "Take off your shoes." So, I took off my shoes and my feet were white. One of the guys rubbed my feet and my nose with snow until some feeling returned. The barracks were not that warm but I was not freezing anymore. After some time, my feet turned black as did the end of my nose. Eventually, I got over the frostbite but I had scarred feet for a long time. There's still evidence to see that, especially my toenails, only two toenails continue to grow, the rest do not grow at all.

And as far as I recall, frostbite was the last disease I had, except for an undiagnosed chest pain that persisted during my last year in captivity when tuberculosis started manifesting in Mukden Camp.

Do you recall what type of food you were given to eat in the Pusan hospital?
When I was in the hospital, I was given the same food that the Japanese were getting, and that had a lot to do with getting my strength back. I don't remember much meat in it. It was mostly a vegetable soup.

This question is not a pleasant one to ask, but I am curious. With little water to drink and almost no food

*to eat before reaching Pusan, how could someone have
a bowel movement?*

For the first nineteen days from the start of the death
march, I had no normal bowel movement, none. And
then for the thirty-two days[43] while I was on that hell-
ship, all I ate was the dried fish in my pockets with a
canteen of water. It's very possible when they hosed me
down at Taiwan, I filled my canteen again. I did get
water again. I didn't turn my canteen loose or leave it
on the ship because I'd have never seen it again. But for
at least thirty-four consecutive days from the time
before I left Manila until after the time I was hospital-
ized in Pusan, no movement.

*Between the Bataan Death March and the hell-ship
journey, can you describe your experience with starvation?*

Of course, the first thing is water. I didn't think
about food or anything else when I was dying of thirst.
Now, once I got enough water, that's when I began to
think about food. I didn't realize the shape that I was in
until removing my clothes in Taiwan. I still had the
same coveralls on and the sleeves were down to here
and the legs were down here *(describing with hand
motion)*.

I did have shoes on my feet, but when I dropped
them and got out of those clothes, I saw that I was
nothing but skin and bones. Normally I weighed one-
hundred fifty-five to one hundred sixty pounds in
peacetime. At the time of the surrender, I was down

---

[43] Jim boarded Tottori Maru in Manila (07OCT1942) and disembarked at Pusan
(08NOV1942) (Map 3).

forty pounds. Then in the prison camps in the Philippines, it kept going down, down and down. When I arrived in Mukden, I was weighed with a Japanese uniform and shoes at ninety-two pounds, and I was still very weak.

At night, the barracks were cold and they gave everybody four blankets to keep warm. I didn't have the strength to cover myself so the guys sleeping next to me covered me with the four blankets. I began to hurt from the weight of the blankets because my bones barely had any flesh. I was in misery for a long time. I don't remember exactly how long it was before I finally got well enough, but at some point they said it was time for me to go to work. So, I started, like everybody else, going to work every day at the factory, which probably was one of the best places of all I had been assigned.

12   Attack by U.S. Planes at Mukden 07DEC1944

It just seemed like the war would never end. Every day was just the same, the Japanese would get us up, line us up, count us at roll call[44], march us to the factory, count us again, and then we went to whatever job we had. That went on day, after day, seven days a week. But one day, the sirens began going off in the city, so the Japanese hurriedly rushed us back to our camp. Normally they checked us as we left the camp, when we arrived at the factory, when we left the factory, and when we got back to the camp, so we were checked four or five times making sure that nothing was carried from the factory to the camp.

But that day, on account of the air raid, they just ran us straight to the camp without being checked, and that's the reason we were not allowed in our barracks. We stayed outside in the little playground we had. We could see a large number of airplanes in flight and headed in our direction since the contrails were visible way up into the sky. There could have been as many as a dozen B-29s. The Japanese say "be nee yuh coos," or B-29 in Japanese speech. We were not familiar with the

---

[44] At daily roll-call, POWs acknowledged presence by pronouncing in Japanese assigned prison numbers. Jim's prison number was 1439, so his name for his Japanese captors was "Ichi-shi-san-kyu".

new American airplanes because they were manufactured after our capture.

Virtually no information reached us in our captivity. But we were thrilled, and after all these years, here came some American planes, which meant, perhaps, that the war was getting close to an end, but not just yet. Their first target was to the left of us, an ammunition factory. I was watching the bombs fall, especially the plane at the end of the formation. It made a kind of unsteady wiggle and hurled three bombs at our camp. One of them hit the brick wall that surrounded the camp, knocking out a big chunk of the wall.

Another one fell smack in the middle of us and the third one hit our barracks, setting it on fire. Eighteen or nineteen POWs were immediately killed[45], including two of my friends[46] Sabo[47] and Mabry[48], while fifty-four were severely wounded. I was within a few feet of those killed and several of those killed were beyond me, further away from the blast than me. That's another close call.

---

[45] Bombs fell on 07DEC1944: U.S. Cpls Ray John Long, Robert Earl Mitchell, Billy Sunday Sutton; US WOs Herbert Wayne Grizzard, Arthur Verlie Lane, Lonnie G Mabry, Frederick Scott Ravin, Thomas Edwin Wall; U.S. Pvts William Eulice Buck, Ulyses Byron Carr, Leon Richard Jette, Edward E Privatsky, Ralph William Roetschke, Alex James Sabo, Leon Skebicki; and UK LCpl John Alford Scholl died on 07DEC. US Cpl John Walter Fleming and US Pvt Kenneth Charles Wood died on 08DEC, and UK Sgt Alfred William Gooby died on 10DEC. (Churchill 14) (mansell.com/pow_resources/camplists/china_hk/mukden/MUKDEN_Civilians_POW_deaths_RG407Bx190.pdf)

[46] USAAC soldiers addressed each other by using their last names.

[47] Sabo, Alex: Rank: Pvt, POW - Bataan Death March survivor, Died: 07DEC1944 in captivity at Mukden Camp, Unit: USAAC 16th Bomb Sqn, 27th Bomb GP, From: GA (May 176)

[48] Mabry, Lonnie: Rank: Radioman 2nd Class, (ASN: 2658522), POW -captured on Corregidor, Died: 07DEC1944 in captivity at Mukden Camp, Unit: US Navy, From: WV (valor.militarytimes.com/hero/303682)

After that, I'd lie on my back and watch our planes drop lots of bombs. While Japanese planes dropped no more than a dozen bombs at a time, the B-29s dropped a ton of bombs. There were many more air raids and we did not have to work until the bombing stopped. A couple of days after the deadly bombing, another big flight formation approached and I was on my back, watching. I could see silver objects flashing in the sky after being released from the planes at very high altitudes. I figured the bombs might hit us again but these bombs went over our heads and struck an airplane factory[49] located behind the camp. I turned around on my back to see the explosions. It scared the devil out of me.

Later on, the B-29s bombed from ten thousand feet, and the Japanese knocked one of them down while I was watching.[50] The plane exploded and the engines fell to the ground. The pilots and crew survived and held in a different camp near us. We fed them from our camp, and eventually we made contact with them.

Describe a typical workday at Mukden Prison Camp.

We were imprisoned at Mukden to provide labor to install the machinery and tools for a Ford truck plant.

---

[49] 108 B-29s flew the mission from Chengtu, China to bomb the Manchuria Airplane Manufacturing Company and an arsenal at Mukden. Seven of the planes were lost. "American Missions Against Mukden."
pacificwrecks.com, Pacific Wrecks, Inc. 1995-2003
(pacificwrecks.com/airfields/manchuria/mukden_north/missions-mukden.html)
[50] One B-29 was downed (07DEC1944), reported as rescued were crew members Kenneth Beckwith, George Brown, John Campbell, Ralph Davidson, Elbert Edwards, Aaron Eldred, Olen Herman, Walter Huss, Benjamin Lipscomb, George Matako, Richard McCormick, Arnold Pope, Daniel Stieber, and Virgil Unruh. "Crew Members of B-29", Mansell.com, Roger Mansell, [n.d.]
(mansell.com/pow_resources/camplists/china_hk/mukden/
B-29_crew_Mukden_1945_b.jpg))

The Ford Motor Company had set up factories full of machinery to be used to assemble trucks but the war broke out and that didn't happen. The Japanese figured that since we were Americans, we could put the equipment together and turn out Ford trucks. But that didn't happen, of course.

There were huge crates of heavy machines and all of the fine parts for the machines to function were in small boxes inside the large crates. We set up all the big machines according to the way the Japanese wanted them. Most of these machines were large and heavy, requiring a strong support base. We dug holes, depending on the size of the machine, in the ground a little bigger than a machine and filled the hole with concrete, which was going to be the base for the machine. Many of the fine little tools, such as dials, calipers, specialty nuts, bolts, and stuff that enabled the machine to function ended up in the concrete. None of the machines were ever operational. I heard once that two little drill presses had been turned out by the POWs. We had these open latrines and the small parts were often dropped in there where the Chinese probably retrieved them when they emptied the honey buckets.

Did the factory have heating?

Yes and no. I remember one day when someone was complaining about the cold. So a Japanese guard came by and said, "Everybody, that's air-cold, step up. Come forward." I thought he said Air Corps. He was saying "air cold," which meant somebody was complaining about being cold. So, I stepped forward because I was in the Air Corps. They took us out and ran us around until we were warmed up. Boy, I made a mistake there.

How many POWs were in Mukden Camp over the three and one-half years you were in captivity?

There were three barracks with double floors, and I can give you a good idea of how many people we had there. In each of the barracks, there were perhaps ten sections and each section held about twenty men, enlisted men downstairs and officers upstairs, so about four-hundred people per building. So, three buildings with four-hundred POWs in each building, twelve-hundred people, pretty close.[51]

Several years ago, you mentioned being held in solitary confinement before you were liberated by the Russian army. What was it like in total isolation?

It all started when we had been working in the lumberyard outside. We got into the factory, went through inspection, and the guards turned us loose in the lumberyard where there was a small shack for us to congregate. On the lumberyard ground were piles of lumber stacked ten feet high. One morning the Japanese were having some sort of maneuver, doing something, in the lumber yard. We walked through, passed by them paying no attention, and entered the shack. The Japanese officer in charge didn't like that so he came into the shack and he was mad. We did not know what he was complaining about so he pulled his saber, shook it, and then left shutting the door behind him. One of the guys in the shack laughed after the door closed, but

[51] On liberation, 1,318 POWs were housed, comprising 280 officers and 1,038 enlisted. (Norwood, Shek 1)

(axpow.org/medsearch/PAC-HOTEN.pdf) "Comprehensive Report of the U.S. Side of the U.S. –Russia Joint Commission on POW/MIAs" (12)

(dpaa.mil/Portals/85/Documents/USRJC/USsideUS-Russia_Joint_Commission_POW-MIAS.pdf)

the officer was listening at the door. He heard our guy laugh so he opened the door and came in again. Now he was really mad, lined all of us up, and started hitting each person in the face. I was standing next to the door and while he was hitting the other guys, I was able to sneak out of the door. He beat everybody in there but he didn't beat me.

When we got to camp, they called out our numbers. Our guy in charge was an Englishman, named Sergeant Lee, who had to turn in the names of the people in the group which included mine because I was part of it, although I didn't get hit. The Japanese questioned us individually and wanted to know what happened. When he got to me, the interpreter said, "Do you think the Japanese had the right to hit you?" When I should have said "Yes, oh yes sir," I said, "I'm not sure." He asked me a few more questions and then came back to me with the same question. Again, I answered the same way, "I'm not sure," and that's when I got whacked, bloodied black eyes, bleeding from inside of my mouth, and bleeding from being hit in my teeth.

They threw me into the brig, and then got me up at six in the morning. I was fed bread and water every third day. The cell walls were made of concrete blocks on three sides and the front wall was two-by-fours with an air space in between each upright. I could see into the other cells across the corridor but the openings to those cells were sort of at an angle, not directly in front of my cell. The concrete floor had a hole to do your thing. I was ordered to stand in the front of the cell from six in the morning until ten at night, day after day after day. The guards patrolled the length of the prison block and would peek through the two-by-fours as they walked by to make sure I was standing. But they only thought I was standing because I could hear the heels of their boots walking back and forth, back and forth. I'd relax when the guard was on the far end of the cell block and by the time he returned to my end, I'd be standing up.

There was a small crack in the roof of my cell that allowed a small amount of light to shine onto the floor. The light appeared on the floor at dawn throughout the day and traveled ever so slowly across the floor until dusk when it disappeared. It seemed forever for that little light to slowly move across the floor from dawn to dusk. When light disappeared after sunset, I knew it would be another two or three hours before they'd let me sleep. It seemed like an eternity watching that light. It was terrible.

There weren't many beatings anymore, none of that, it's the complete isolation. I could see the guys in their cells across the corridor. We learned to do the alphabet with our fingers and were able to communicate. Oh, simple, we spelled words with our fingers. Yeah, like Q and P. It's so easy to remember and simple to use. Our trial had not started, so we were collaborating, getting our story the same, before we'd go to trial. But there was no reason for the guard to hit me. I was right when I said he didn't have the right to hit me.

I was in solitary for nineteen days and released shortly before the war ended and freedom, on August 15, 1945, my birthday.

What was the worst camp of your captivity; O'Donnell, Gapan, Cabanatuan or Mukden?

O'Donnell, the first one, O'Donnell, Oh man, the disease, primarily dysentery, as I said earlier, was the big killer. The stricken passed blood and mucus, and the flies were over everything. Those poor guys were lying there naked, thousands of flies in their eyes, their mouths, and everywhere else. You talk about a bad place. I don't know if what I had was dysentery. All I know is that I had loose bowels and I ate those leaves from a little bush.

On August 15, 1945, the day that the Armistice was announced, what was it like leading up to the announcement on your birthday?

In the days before the Armistice, we were still in the routine of going to the factory early in the morning. The Japanese guards would still get us up at the crack of dawn and we worked until it was time to return to the barracks before dark.

One morning, we were going to the factory and all of a sudden we saw a strange plane flying low, perhaps no more than a thousand feet above the ground. It was easily seen, parachutes were deployed and people were jumping out of the plane.[52] I'd never seen a plane[53] like that, so my impression was that it wasn't one of ours. It didn't look like a Japanese plane that I'd ever seen. It was a good-sized plane with two engines. Nevertheless, we went to the factory, but during the day I was think-

---

[52] A six member Office of Strategic Services (OSS) team parachuted into Mukden (16AUG1945), contacted Japanese camp commandant, Colonel Genji Matsuda, to coordinate evacuation of the camp, and to contact and release General Wainwright. (Streifer 22, 23)

[53] A B-24 bomber, piloted by Lt. Paul Hallberg, deployed the team and 17 cargo parachutes, pulled back controls to avoid a collision with a Japanese kamikaze pilot in a fighter plane. (Streifer 22)

ing, "Maybe that was a German plane." It had been rumored around the camp that Germany had fallen, so I figured, "It's a German plane, some Germans escaped and were coming to Manchuria."

That evening when we got back into camp, the guards lined us up to be searched, and as we walked toward our barracks, we noticed six guys standing against the brick wall. I figured that my first impression of them during the day was correct, that they were Germans because I didn't recognize the clothes they were wearing. But when one of them[54] made this sign, we knew what it was, the O.K. sign, we knew that something was up.

At the beginning of the next day, the routine was the same as always. The guards searched us in the morning, turned us loose in camp, and then at the end of the day they searched us again. When it was almost dark, the person assigned would bring soup to the barracks, we'd eat, and then the lights were turned off.

But on that night, the guards didn't come to turn off the lights, and pretty soon we knew something was up. Instead of spending the night in the barracks, everybody just spent the night roaming around outside, since no guards were present. Then someone was able to see what was going on between the Japanese and those guys who were standing at the wall, they could see that they were arguing with our Japanese camp com-

---

[54] OSS team (a.k.a. Cardinal) comprised Major James T. Hennessy (Team leader), Major Robert F. Lamar (physician), Technician Edward A. Starz (radio operator), S/Sgt Harold "Hal" B. Leith (Russian and Chinese linguist), Sgt Fumio Kido (2nd generation Japanese interpreter), and Cheng Shih-wu (Chinese interpreter). (Streifer 22)

mander.[55] It wasn't until the next day that we found out that an armistice had been signed. Soon, one of our generals, General Parker,[56] who was in charge of the camp, told us, "The war is over, you are back in the army, and you're not going to treat the Japanese like they treated us."

But we did have that opportunity because very soon, the Russians arrived, having recently declared war on Japan.[57] There was a lot of bombing in that area, but none close to us. The Russians came to the gate of the POW camp. I do not remember if they knocked it down or had the Japanese open it or what, but they're the ones that came in with their general. He stood up on something, it was not a stool, but he was standing on something and began to give us a talk. He was speaking in Russian but luckily one of our POWs was born somewhere in the region of Russia and was fluent in their language. So, he was able to be the interpreter. And of course, the Russian general[58] was bragging, claiming he had talked to Eisenhower. Most of us did

---

[55] Colonel Matsuda was tried in Shanghai after the war and sentenced to 7 years imprisonment for his crimes. "Matsuda to Stand Trial Article", C.W. Felps Collection, University of Virginia Law Library

(imtfe.law.virginia.edu/collections/phelps-collection/1/1/matsuda-stand-trial-news-article)

[56] Major General George M. Parker, Jr. arrived in Mukden Camp from a POW camp in China to become the senior American officer (21MAY1945). (Streifer 23) (Norwood, Shek 1) (axpow.org/medsearch/PAC-HOTEN.pdf)

[57] The Soviet Union declared war on Japan (08AUG1945) and attacked Japanese-occupied Manchuria.

[58] Several Russian officers assisted the American POW contact team with the evacuation by procuring transportation. Russian General Pritula was recommended for American decorations. "Comprehensive Report of the U.S. Side of the U.S. –Russia Joint Commission on POW/MIAs" (p13)

(dpaa.mil/Portals/85/Documents/USRJC/USsideUS-Russia_Joint_Commission_POW-MIAS.pdf)

not know who Eisenhower was at the time. "Oh, yeah," I told him, "I've covered and I've gone across rivers, through forests and deserts and over mountains to get here to relieve you."

We knew he was lying, but we would cheer him every time he'd open his mouth.

Then he had all the Japanese guards come out and stand in the small parade ground. He lined them up and then he got the same number of POWs to stand facing them. We were only about twenty feet across from each other. They were here and we were there *(motioning with his hands)*. Well, I was one of the guards selected (Photo 10). We had rifles, and I know the Russians wanted us to shoot them. But it didn't happen.

The Russians called it *changing-of-the-guards*. When they saw we weren't going to do anything, they then took the Japanese guards somewhere, perhaps to the guard house. Finally, we were allowed to roam. We could go out, go to the city, and do whatever we wanted to do. We were free.

Photo 10: From Right to left; Jim standing guard with a Russian issued rifle, unknown ex-POW guard with a pistol in his belt, Mukden Prison Camp Commander Colonel Genji Matsuda, Australian Recovery Team Officer, Japanese interpreter.

In the meantime, we were being supplied by air. The big B-29s were dropping food, clothes, and everything else to us right into the camp, but it was dangerous. The contents were in barrels, the barrels were heavy, and they'd tear loose from the parachutes. The parachute would open and the barrel would tear it apart.

In one of the camps, a barrel fell on one of our guys and killed him. They were hitting the roofs of buildings and punching holes through them.[59] That was not working well so they dropped walkie-talkies and some of the guys figured out how to use them and communicate with the airmen in the planes. That's when they

---

[59] (Streifer 24)

started dropping the barrels outside the camp. But that led to other problems because the Chinese locals living outside the camp wanted the contents as much as we did, but we did get enough to eat.

At the USS Kidd Museum,[60] *there is a display encasing a photo of you, your military uniform, and a Japanese Samurai sword. What is the story of the sword, your connection to it?*

As I mentioned, we were free to roam, go into the town, and that's when I started looking for a souvenir. I wanted a Japanese saber as a symbol to show that we were the victors and a saber[61] would best indicate that.

So, I walked downtown near the railroad station where trains were arriving and leaving with loads of Russians, coming in and going out. I was by myself looking for a saber but there were no sabers to be found. I thought, perhaps, the Japanese had already been disarmed. So that approach didn't work and I walked back to the camp.

But soon I left again with a friend to continue the hunt for sabers. We went to another nearby area, a place like an industrial site, and a worker told us where a warehouse was full of sabers that the Russians had already collected. He said, "Why don't you go there and get one?" so we did, only to find that a Russian was guarding the warehouse. He could speak a little English so I asked him if we could each have a saber.

---

[60] A National Historic Landmark docked on the Mississippi River in Baton Rouge, LA.

[61] A Samurai sword, used by early Japanese warriors became a status symbol, a family heirloom, and national treasure.
(worldhistory.org/Samurai_Sword/)

He said emphatically, "Oh no, no. There has been an inventory and if they find some are missing, I will be in trouble." He just didn't want to give us anything, of all those sabers probably 100 or more, so we left and went back into camp.

But the next day, another friend of mine, Sergeant Ken Farmer,[62] and I resumed the search for sabers. So, Ken and I got on a bicycle, left the camp, and pedaled way out into the countryside. Marching toward us was a huge column of Japanese soldiers. When they got close to us, Ken noticed that they still had their sabers strapped to their waist. So, he approached one of the soldiers in the column and said to him demandingly, "Give me that!" pointing to his saber. So, the guy obediently unbuckled and threw it off the side. Then Ken said to another soldier in a similar commanding gesture, "Give me that!" So, the whole column thought we were disarming them. We didn't do anything more as they continued to cast their sabers in a pile off the side of the road. They just kept coming and throwing their sabers on the pile.

We didn't see this at first, but pretty soon this Japanese soldier on horseback, perhaps the commander of the column of soldiers, came toward us riding full speed ahead with his saber out. He must have been wondering "What in the world is going on?" and he was extremely mad because the whole column had stopped. Ken, who was a feisty little guy and small in

[62] Farmer, Kenneth L: Rank: Sgt, Service: 7002784, POW - Bataan Death March and Mukden Camp survivor, Liberated: 15AUG1945, Unit: USAAC 16th Bomb Sqn, 27th Bomb GP, From: Leeds, AL.
(obituaries.newsaegis.com/obituary/kenneth-farmer-sr-755719271)
(valor.militarytimes.com/hero/355205)

stature, grabbed one of the sabers from the pile and boldly approached the guy on the horse. Now, I am not exactly sure of his words, but it was more or less, "If you don't get the hell out of here I'm going to cut your horse's head off and your head as well." It worked, the column resumed their march led by the guy on his horse and we collected at least thirty sabers.

In hindsight, I think the Japanese commander on the horse probably thought we were Russian soldiers who were ordered to disarm Japanese soldiers. I say this for two reasons: first, the Japanese surrendered to the Russians on August 19 and were disarming Japanese soldiers around Mukden, and second, the commander on the horse would not have known the difference between an American and a Russian soldier. He thought we were Russian soldiers under orders, otherwise he would not have allowed us to take those swords.

Momentarily we faced another problem. How to carry thirty sabers back to the camp on a bicycle? But soon the issue was resolved. A Chinese farmer came along with a flatbed cart pulled by a horse. We stopped him, loaded his cart with sabers, and hired him to carry them back to the camp.

I selected one saber (Photo 11), Ken took one, and Herbie took two of them. I am pretty sure that anyone from Mukden who returned home with a saber had one of the thirty or so that we brought back to the camp.

So, we had our sabers but had to watch it. I was with the last bunch that left Mukden, the last truck out of

Photo 11: Jim holding his Japanese Samurai Sword in his living room.

the camp.[63] When we got to the boat[64] waiting at Port Arthur[65], the skipper wouldn't let us aboard unless we turned in our sabers. Other guys had rifles, pistols, and stuff like that. But we said, "No, we're not getting on without our stuff, so send us another ship." The skipper finally relented, and allowed us to board, and I slept with that thing, never let it go. The only time I was separated from my saber was aboard the Colbert when it hit that mine. After the typhoon passed, I left topside and went back to my bunk to get it.

[63] Jim left Mukden Camp (11SEP1945) and arrived by train in Port Arthur, China. (Map 3).

[64] USS Colbert voyaged to Port Arthur to embark former American POWs held at Mukden (Map 3).

[65] Port Arthur (a.k.a. Dalian or Dairen) is located on southern tip of a peninsula in the north Yellow Sea between China and North Korea. During the war, the port was known to Americans as 'Port Arthur'.

Where was Ken Farmer from?

I am not completely sure but he may have been born in Leeds, Alabama. After the war, we spent some time together. Ken had a son[66] who joined the army and became a general. We stayed in touch.

---

[66] Wikipedia Editors. "Kenneth L. Farmer Jr.", 22NOV2023 (en.wikipedia.org/wiki/Kenneth_L._Farmer_Jr.)

13 USS Colbert Struck by a Mine
16SEP1945

Photo 12: General Wainwright broadcasting surrender Instructions (MAY1942)

At the time we left Mukden Camp, I do not know how many were listed to be picked up at Port Arthur. The first people leaving Mukden were the high-ranking civilians and military personnel and the highest rank was General Wainwright (Photo 12) who was held in captivity about one-hundred miles north of Mukden[67].

---

[67] Colonel Matsuda informed the OSS team that General Wainwright was in Sian. Team members Leith and Lamar boarded a train, arrived in Sian, met generals King, Wainwright, and their party of POW captives. (Streifer 23)

Originally, most of the highest-ranking officers were held in Taiwan, but as the American forces got closer to Taiwan, the Japanese moved the prisoners to Mukden. Many American airplanes were coming and going. The high-ranking people were the first to be flown out, followed by the sick to a hospital ship that was docked in Port Arthur, I think. I was in one of the last groups that departed and do not remember the number in our count.[68] No POWs remained in the camp by the time I left. The Russians provided train transport for us to Port Arthur, China.

When we arrived at the harbor and boarded the ship, the USS Colbert, we pulled anchor and were on our way to Okinawa. In the daytime, several floating mines were spotted and sailors on board the Colbert sunk them with machine guns.

After four days at sea we arrived in Buckner Bay[69] an hour or two before dark, but the ship started rocking due to rough seas and the Colbert (Photo 13) was ordered to leave the bay and head back to sea because Typhoon Ursula was heading directly for Okinawa. It was dark by the time we were back out to sea. The ship seemed stable. I was assigned a top bunk at the top of the four levels and fell asleep. At four o'clock in the morning, I heard a loud, terrific bang that shook the ship. The lights went out, the sea was rough, when the Colbert struck a mine (Photo 14) flooding the engine

---

[68] On 10SEP1945, 750 ex-POWs left by train for Port Arthur, the remaining 280 ex-prisoners departed the next day. Mukden Camp resumed its role as prison for 5,000 Japanese soldiers captured by the Russians. (Streifer 25)

[69] A bay located on the southern coast of Okinawa, was a key operating port for the U.S. fleet (Map 3).

Photo 13: USS Colbert was a U.S. Navy transport ship in service (1945-1946).

Photo 14: USS Colbert dry-docked at Okinawa. During Typhoon Ursula (17SEP1945), the ship struck a floating mine 100 miles east of Okinawa causing the death of several men including Jim's friend, William Frising, the only POW aboard who died in the explosion.

room and killing several sailors and one POW.[70] With
the seas fifty feet high, in total darkness, and without
power, sailors came through carrying lights and told us
to grab life preservers. I took one, headed to the top
side, and prepared to abandon ship.

After getting topside there were problems. I held on
to anything I could grasp, or be thrown off the ship. It
was the wind, a typhoon, and the rain was horizontal.
Working my way around the ship holding on to pipes, I
settled next to a bulkhead but still held on to the nearby
pipes. I figured that eventually I would get too tired,
release my grip, and be thrown off. So, using the life
preserver belt I tied myself to one of the pipes and spent
the next 3 or 4 hours hanging on until the storm finally
passed. There was twilight, although the sun had not
yet come up, but there was enough light to see and
about that time the captain released a message that we
were only one-hundred miles from Okinawa. He was
trying to calm us down, I thought.

On the third day, when the seas started to calm, a big
transport about the same size as our ship pulled aside
the Colbert and threw a line to our crew thinking they
could tow the Colbert into Okinawa, but it didn't
work. They couldn't pull us, so our crew cut them loose
and they took off.

The next day I was on deck. In the distance, I could
see this little boat coming, but couldn't imagine why it
was coming for us because it was so tiny. It turned out
to be a small, powerful tugboat. Its crew threw a line to
our crew, hooked us up, and that little boat had enough

---

[70] Accounts vary as to the exact number of men who died (16SEP1945).

power to tow us to Okinawa. There, we got off the ship and could see the huge gaping hole in the side. The Colbert was a new ship, only a couple of years old. If we'd been on an older ship, the mine would have sunk us. But that's one thing that saved us, the fact that we were in a more modern, good, and well-built ship.

14 Flight to Manila in a B-24 Bomb Bay OCT1945

When we got off the Colbert in Okinawa, they took us to the base[71] and fed us. The next morning, they took us to the parade ground and treated us to an air show where there were chairs for us to sit. And all of a sudden, a fighter plane came. There are hills around the base, and the fighter plane zoomed down and over, only a couple of hundred feet from where we were sitting. Then another one zoomed right behind the first, then another behind the second one, and yet another behind the last one where the planes zooming by got lower and lower to the ground. There were perhaps four planes making circles and lower and lower to the ground with each pass. I thought to myself, "Stop it. You're going to get killed. We've seen enough." Then one solo plane zoomed by and hit the top of the flagpole, sending a sound of ripping metal and bending the flagpole into a 'C'.

Later on, I read an account of the storm, the typhoon on Okinawa, describing the winds as so strong that they bent the flagpole. But that was not right. I saw what bent the flagpole. There's no way in the world that wind could do that. But certainly, the typhoon in

---

[71] Japanese airport Yara Hikojo on Okinawa was later renamed Kadena Air Base.

Okinawa sunk a lot of ships, and many sailors were lost.

What would you estimate the number of days it took to get to Okinawa after the mine explosion?

Four days, maybe longer, for the seas to calm down, for help to arrive, and for that small tug to tie on and pulled us in. I'd like to say more about the damage from the mine explosion as far as people were concerned. I heard that eight of the sailors in the engine room were killed when the mine exploded. It created such a big hole that some seamen had been washed out, which makes sense. One POW was killed in the explosion. He was a good friend of mine, William Frising.[72] In Mukden, he was known as One Eye because he had developed trouble with his eyes where the lens of each of his eyes turned milky. It was a common problem among POWs, probably due to vitamin deficiency, but eventually, the problem would disappear for most people, but not for poor William. One of his eyes healed, but one stayed milky.

That evening, after the air show, we met the pilots for dinner and that's when we were told that the pilot whose plane struck the flagpole made it safely back to base.

The next morning they took us to the airfield where four B-24s were waiting to take us to Manila. They were to transport us in the bomb bay section[73] of each

---

[72] William Frising: Rank: PFC, Service: 297135; POW - Mukden Camp survivor, Liberated:15AUG1945, Died: 19SEP1945 aboard USS Colbert, Unit: USMC Co 4th Marines, From: Richmond Hill NYC.

[73] Four B-24 Liberators departed Okinawa (27SEP1945) to ferry U.S. POWs to Clark Airfield, Philippines. (Map 3)

plane. The seating arrangements in the bomb bays were temporary seats made out of a one by twelve *(1 inch thick by 12 inch wide board)* for the length of the bomb bay section. Each of two benches held ten to twelve people. They instructed us to select a plane so I jumped on the third plane. The four planes were filled with POWs. They closed the bomb bay doors and took off.

Now I didn't see this, but I later found out that it did happen. During the flight one of the planes' bomb bay doors accidently opened[74] and sucked the POWs out, dropping them in the sea. I could easily see why it happened because we were seated at the edge of the opening. We weren't holding on to anything and there was no way in the world that you wouldn't fall out if the door opened.

Later on, my wife and I heard from Senator Jesse Knowles,[75] who said he saw it happen. Jesse may have been sitting in the copilot seat, because the bomb bay section was closed in. At a later convention, one of our officers, Lieutenant Harrelson[76], who was also on one of the planes, said he saw it happen. There is at least one reference of the event in books I've read, but I have never seen an official military record that mentions this.

---

[74] (Allen 182)

[75] Knowles, Jesse Monroe: Rank: Sgt, POW - Bataan Death March and Mukden Camp survivor, Liberated: 15AUG1945; Unit: 16th Bomb Sqn, 27th Bomb GP, From: Calcasieu Parish, LA

[76] Harrelson, Jay B: Rank: 2nd Lt, Service: O&411831, POW - Bataan Death March and Mukden Camp survivor, Liberated: 15AUG1945, Unit: USACC 16th Bomb Sqn, 27th Bomb GP, From Crossville, AL

(west-point.org/family/japanese-pow/EricksonCSV.htm)

How did you feel to be free after three and one-half years and to be on your way home after almost five years?

It was sometime in September when we finally arrived in Manila (Map 3). I cannot remember the exact date, but we were sent to a preparation center to send us home. There was a bulletin board that we had to watch for our name and the ship to which we would be assigned to get home. We were scattered and turned loose with a larger crowd, not just with POWs as a group. I watched the bulletin board carefully for my name to appear, and finally I was brought to the ship that would bring me home.

On the ship, I was with a lot of sailors and other people, not with a group of POWs. When I arrived in San Francisco, they knew I was POW. They must have had a manifest of people arriving and I was probably pointed out as a POW. They did pull me out of the bunch, put me in a truck, and brought me to Letterman General Hospital,[77] where they took my clothes and put me in pajamas. That's where I stayed for a couple of weeks; of course, they gave me a good examination.

Later, still in PJs, they put us on a hospital train with no seats, only beds, and patients. We were still in beds when we arrived at Brooks General[78] in San Antonio where I stayed for quite a while. It was here that I shared with the doctors that I still had a medical problem. I explained that five or six months before the

---

[77] A U.S. Army hospital located in the Presidio of San Francisco, CA, decommissioned in 1994.

[78] A convalescent unit accommodated war casualties, now the Brooke Army Medical Center.

(Japanese) surrender, I started having pain in the center of my chest. At first, I thought it might be a result of the pneumonia I had, from which I had recovered, and that was probably almost three years back. But I could take a deep breath and no pain. And I figured it wasn't my heart because when I kind of crunched my arms like this, it was really painful. It felt like it was in my breastbone. They checked my heart, lungs, and all that kind of stuff. They weren't sure what it was. They kept me for a while but finally, they told me I could go home. They put me on a train and that's when I met my friend, Herbie Lanclos, from Lafayette[79] who was going home at the same time. He lived in Lafayette and I lived in Eunice but we stopped in Crowley to spend the night in a hotel because I wanted to get a haircut and look good when I got home, having been away for four and a half years. I don't know why Herbie stopped in Crowley other than he wanted to stay with me.

The next morning, I went to a barbershop for a haircut, only one barber at this shop, sat in the chair, and he began cutting my hair. He started talking about the local boys who were in the war and said, "There's this one family," and described where they lived. He did not remember the family name but said there were four in the service, and that two in Europe had been killed, one was a prisoner of the Japanese, and the fourth one was in the Pacific getting ready to invade Japan. And right off the bat, I knew that had to be my family, the way he described everything. I kind of froze

---

[79] Crowley, Eunice, Opelousas, and Lafayette are cities in southwest Louisiana.

for a while. He finished cutting my hair. I paid him, and left. He didn't know that I was the POW.

I told Herbie about what I had just learned, and then called my half-sister who lived in Eunice, to come to Crowley and pick us up. When my half-sister arrived, she immediately said to me, "Andrew[80] and Stephen,"[81] but I interrupted her and replied, "I already know." It was true what I had assumed. So, I asked her if we could drive to Lafayette to bring Herbie home rather than him having to take the train. So we did, stopped at his house, and waited while he got out of the car and walked to his home. His family came out, joyfully hugging Herbie. We watched them for a few moments then drove to Eunice through Opelousas, and then went to the farm, my boyhood home.

My parents, brothers, and sisters were waiting for me. My poor mother was in tears, but her first words were about my older brother, who was her favorite. She started saying, we called him "B" and she started saying, "B." And I said, "Mama, I know," but she was broken up. It wasn't the tears of joy that I expected; it was just tears of sorrow. My father was very quiet, we just shook hands. They called me "Pat", so he just said, "Pat." All he said was, "Pat." I didn't recognize any of my half-sister's three young kids. I didn't recognize them at all. I recognized my brother, Al, but later my youngest sister, Joanne, said she didn't remember me. I

[80]Bollich, Andrew Leo: Rank: 2nd Lt, Service #O-791841, KIA: 27JUN1943, Location: Sardinia, Unit: 319th Fighter Sqn, 325th Fighter GP: From: Mowata, Acadia Parish, LA (honorstates.org/profiles/478718/)

[81]Bollich, Stephen: Rank: 2nd Lt, Service # O-688301, DND: 27MAR1944, Location: Foggia Italy, Unit: 758th Bomb Sqn, 459th Bomb GP, From: Mowata, Acadia Parish, LA (honorstates.org/profiles/478719/)

was a stranger. That didn't go very well for me to get home, because I just felt like a stranger. All the while I was a POW, I kept thinking about the happy times that I had at home, "When I get back, I'm going to have a happy time with my brothers. We're going to go swimming in the bayou," and all that stuff. Then to get home and found out they were dead, and I didn't even know my family anymore. My poor parents were devastated, and I couldn't wait to leave the place, and it's never been home since. That's the way it was.

Were you discharged from the Army when you got home?

I was home but not officially discharged. I was still in the service and was supposed to go back to San Antonio for the discharge, but that was changed sometime during the four weeks after I got home. They told me I had to travel to Hattiesburg, Mississippi to be discharged. They gave me a train ticket where so many people were waiting to get on the train. The only seat available was in the baggage car, so I sat on baggage to Hattiesburg. But I was determined to get on that train.

I arrived in Hattiesburg at night to find a large number of empty tents for the soldiers being discharged. I was told, "Go find a tent," so I did. There was no food to eat, only a tent. I needed to use the latrine before sleeping. Inside the latrine, beside me, were three drunken Puerto Ricans complaining about the lack of attention being given to them. They felt discriminated against by people like me. Although they did not directly threaten me, I felt threatened because of their behavior. When I went back to my bunk in the tent, there were a bunch of empty beer bottles where the guys ahead of me had been celebrating before they were kicked out. I grabbed one of the beer bottles to use as a club, just in case somebody came in, and I'd have to defend myself, but nothing happened. Perhaps I was being overly cautious.

The next morning, I went to be discharged and that was it, on my own, and no transportation offered to get home. So, I got with four other people that were being discharged and we hired a taxi that took us to New Orleans. From New Orleans, I took a bus to get to Eunice and that was it. I was out.

One last question: was your chest pain ever diagnosed after you left the San Antonio hospital?

No diagnosis, but it was not TB. The doctor said I could stay in San Antonio, be treated until it got better, or I could be discharged. So, I went for the discharge, got home, applied for the G.I. Bill to start college, and saw a VA doctor in Lafayette. He gave me two bottles of huge vitamin tablets, the size of horse pills, and after four months the pain went away, while I was in college.

So, luckily for me, almost immediately after my discharge, I was approved for the G.I. Bill, and the semester was scheduled to start at SLI,[82] and that's why I was able to leave and go to a school. I left home for the last time, feeling sorry for my parents. I knew they appreciated me being home and surviving the war, but then I had to leave them again so soon. I very seldom went back home and it kept playing on my mind that maybe I ought to do more, but that's the way it was.

---

[82] Acronym for Southwestern Louisiana Institute, now University of Louisiana.

I finished college and went on to do graduate work in New Mexico, met Celia and got married. After all my education, I got a good job, had a wonderful wife and two kids. We had three children but the first child died in infancy. My perfect family; married well, have grand-kids, and up to this point, enjoyed my home and my work. I was a geologist and worked for thirty-six years. I've been retired now for thirty-seven, had a good life, and still have a good life.

Epilogue

Today, Jim lives alone in the home he built in 1955. His two daughters, Sally Bru and Melinda Gilbert, call him every morning. They visit him frequently, often with his five grand-children and seven great-grand-children. His eyesight is sharp and his hearing reasonably acute with the use of hearing aids. He is a voracious reader of non-fictional works of science and history. Recently, he compiled and self-published an academic geology manual, *Interpreting the Subsurface Geology of the Gulf of Mexico Basin*, to be given to the University of Louisiana Geology Department for first-year students to learn some of the fundamentals of local geology. Jim continues to paint on canvas, and grows milkweed for Monarch butterflies to prosper.

During retirement he developed friendships with U.S. Representatives Clay Higgins and Charles Boustany, Louisiana Senator Jesse Knowles, other elected and government officials, USMC Major General Bob Hollingsworth, USA Brigadier General John Sherman Crow, USMC SSGT Ronald Crowley, USAF SGT Karen McCook Crowley, other military leaders and veterans, civic leaders and civilians. His military uniform, commendation medals and ribbons, and Samurai sword acquired after his liberation at Mukden are displayed in the USS Kidd Museum. In 2019 he was awarded the Congressional Gold Medal for his military service in the Philippines.

References

Allen, Oliver. *Abandoned on Bataan: One Man's Story of Survival*. Boerne, Texas, Crimson House Entertainment and Publishing, 2002.

Browne , Allen R. "USA vs Toshio Tsuneyoshi". USA Hq 8th Army. Mansell.com, Roger Mansell, 24MAY1949.

Churchill, N.E. "Mukden Death Records". Philippines Archive Collection, 21FEB1944.

Cox, Samuel J. "H-057-1: Operations Downfall and Ketsugo – NOV1945". *Naval History and Heritage Command*, history.navy.mil, U.S. Navy, JAN2021.

May, Mary Cathrin. The Steadfast Line: The Story of the 27th Bombardment Group. Self-published, 2003.

McManus, John C. "Andersonville of the Pacific". *National Endowment of the Humanities*, 31JUL2019.

Moody, Samuel B. *Reprieve from Hell*. Orlando, Florida, [n.p.], 1961.

Norman, Elizabeth M. and Norman, Michael. "Bataan Death March". *Encyclopedia Britannica*, 08SEP2023, (https://britannica.com/event/Bataan-Death-March. Accessed 22SEP2023).

Norwood, James I, Shek, Emily L. "POW Camps in Areas other than the Four Principal Islands of

Japan". *American Prisoner of War Information Bureau*, 31JUL1946.

Streifer, Bill. "OSS in Manchuria: Operation Cardinal". *The OSS Society Journal,* Summer/Fall 2010, (https://www.academia.edu/1055900/Operation_Cardinal_OSS_in_Manchuria)

"Comprehensive Report of the U.S. Side of the U.S. Russia Joint Commission POW/MIAs". Russia Joint Commission on POW/MIA Affairs, 17JUN1996.

Appendix A: James Bollich - Commendations, Awards, and Books

Military Commendations

1. Bronze Star
2. Purple Heart
3. POW Medal
4. President Unit Citation with two Oak-leaf Clusters
5. American Campaign Medal
6. American Defense Service Medal with one Bronze Star
7. Army Good Conduct Medal
8. Asiatic-Pacific medal with two Bronze Stars
9. WWII Victory Medal
10. Philippine Defense Medal
11. Philippine Independence Medal
12. Philippine Liberation Medal
13. Philippine President's Medal

Additional Awards

- The National Society of the Sons of the American Revolution Bronze Good Citizenship Award - 1993
- The National Society of the Daughters of the American Revolution DAR Medal of Honor - 1999
- St. Edmund High School Distinguished Alumni Award – 2003

- Induction into The Louisiana Veterans Hall of Honor at the USS Kidd Veterans Memorial - 2005

- Knights of Columbus Msgr. Fernand Gouaux Assembly No.2199 Civic Award – 2012

- Acadian Museum Living Legends, Erath, Louisiana - 2014

Authored Books: Nonfiction

A Soldier's Journal (1ˢᵗ Edition) – ISBN-13: 978-0-8062-4507-2, ISBN: 0-8062-4507-7, published 1993 by Carlton Press, Inc., New York NY

A Soldier's Journal (2ⁿᵈ Edition) – ISBN-13: 978-1-58980-167-7, ISBN: 0-9643275-3-8, self-published 1993

Bataan Death March: A Soldier's Story - ISBN-13: 978-1-4556-0060-1, ISBN: 1-4556-0060-1, copyright 1993 (previously titled A Soldier's Journal), First Pelican Publishing Company first edition 2003, second printing 2012

Young James of Acadiana – ISBN-13: 978-0-9643275-0-4, ISBN: 0-9643275-0-3, self-published 1994

Young James to Jim - ISBN-13: 978-0-9643275-1-1, ISBN: 0-9643275-1-1, self-published 1996

White Cotton Over Black Gold - ISBN-13: 978-0-9643275-2-8, ISBN: 0-9643275-2-X, self-published 1998

Missing in Action, WWII: Mission No.70 - ISBN-13: 978-0-9643275-4-2, ISBN: 0-9643275-4-6, self-published 1998

From Buggies 1921 to Jets 2015 – no ISBN, self-published in 2015

Authored Books: Fiction

Innocents at War – ISBN: 0-9643275-5-4, self-published 2000

Still Miles to Go: Acadie' to Louisiana - ISBN-13: 978-0-9643275-5-9, ISBN: 0-9643275-5-4, self-published 2004

Off to Amerika – ISBN: 0-9643275-6-2, converted 978-0-9643275-6-6, self-published 2005

Rebel Grandfather - ISBN-13: 978-0-9643275-7-3, ISBN: 0-9643275-7-0, self-published 2007

Escaped – ISBN: 0-9643275-8-9, self-published 2011

The Search – ISBN: 978-0-692-67661-5, self-published 2016

Appendix B: James Bollich (POW# 1439)
Chronology of Events 1940-46

24AUG1940	Enlisted at Barksdale Field, Shreveport LA, USAAC 16th Bombardment Squadron, 27 Bomb Group, Service # 14014589
21NOV1941	Arrived in Manila aboard SS Coolidge from San Francisco via Hawaii
07DEC1941	Pearl Harbor attacked by Japan
08DEC1941	US declared war on Japan
09DEC1941	Nichols Field bombed, south of Manila in Pasay, Luzon
23DEC1941	Arrived in Lepa, Batangas
25DEC1941	Arrived on Bataan Peninsula
11MAR1942	General MacArthur left Corregidor
01 or 02 APR1942	**#1 Both Running for the Foxhole**, retrieves compass
06APR1942	**#2 Bombing at Mariveles**
08APR1942	Bataan Fell, Major General King surrendered
09APR1942	Bataan Death March began at Mariveles airstrip
10APR1942	**#3 Rushing the Water Well**
10APR1942	**#4 Saved by Friend**
10/11APR1942	**#5 Beer Bottle in Nipa Hut**
14APR1942	**#6 Full Canteen on a Ledge**, arrived in San Fernando
~17-18APR1942	Arrived in Camp O'Donnell, assigned to burial detail
~19APR-05MAY1942	**#7 Cure for Dysentery**

05MAY1942	**#8 Out of O'Donnell on Work Detail**
05MAY1942	In San Fernando on way to build Gapan Bridge
06MAY1942	Corregidor fell, Wainwright captured, sent into captivity at Sian, Manchuria
08MAY1942	Gapan Bridge detail began
29JUN1942	Gapan Bridge detail ended, arrived in Cabanatuan
01AUG1942, 0000h	George Bramlett listed as MIA
06OCT1942:	Left Cabanatuan, hiked 8 miles to train
06OCT1942, 0930h	Left on train for Manila
06OCT1942, 1600h	Arrived in Manila
07OCT1942	Boarded Tottori Maru, Manila Pier 7, at sea 32 days (07OCT-08NOV1942)
08OCT1942, 0700h	Tottori Maru* – Pulled anchor from Pier 7
09OCT1942, 0800h	USS Spearfish fired 3 torpedoes at Tottori Maru
09OCT1942	**#9 Attacked by U.S. Submarine**
10OCT1942	Tottori Maru* - Arrived in Takau, Taiwan, POWs stay on ship
12OCT1942	Tottori Maru* - Departed Takau
16OCT1942	Tottori Maru* - Stayed only 1 day at sea (unknown reason)
17OCT1942, 0600h	Tottori Maru* - Returned to Takau
18OCT1942, 0800h	Tottori Maru* - Left Takau for Mako island (Japan Imperial Navy Guard District)
19OCT1942	Tottori Maru* - Arrived in Mako
21OCT1942	Tottori Maru* - Buried 2 men at sea

26OCT1942	Tottori Maru* - Departed Mako
27OCT1942	Tottori Maru* - Arrived at Takau
28OCT1942	Tottori Maru* - POWs disembarked, hosed down, and embarked.
30OCT1942	Tottori Maru* – Left Takau for Mako
30OCT1942	Tottori Maru* - Departed Mako with convoy en route for Pusan
31OCT1942	Tottori Maru* - Buried 1 man at sea
03NOV1942	Tottori Maru* - Buried 2 men at sea
07NOV1942	Tottori Maru* - Buried 1 man at sea
08NOV1942	Tottori Maru* - Anchored at Pusan after 32 days, POWs disembarked
08NOV1942	**#10: Near Death at Pusan**
11NOV1942	Healthier POWs, but not Jim, arrived at Mukden via train from Pusan
11NOV1942	Tottori Maru* - Arrived at Osaka, disembarked POWs, 30 POWs died aboard
~15DEC1942 (?)	Left Pusan for Mukden by train with cremated POW remains to be interred at Mukden Camp
23FEB1943	Buried 80 men at Mukden
23JUN1943	Three POWs escaped from Mukden; Meringolo, Chastain, Pallioti
10JUL1943	Meringolo, Chastain, Pallioti captured
31JUL1943	Meringolo, Chastain, Pallioti executed
29JUL1943	Moved to new camp (Mukden), hid compass under barrack floor
07DEC1944, 10-1230h	Allied air raid; 86 planes, 3 bombs, 19 killed including Sabo and Mabry, ~54 casualties
07DEC1944	**#11 Attacked by U.S. Planes at Mukden**
JUL/AUG1945	Solitary confinement (19 days)
15AUG1945	Turned 24 years old, Mukden Camp POWs freed

16AUG1945	6-man OSS Team arrived; OSS man gave Jim a thumbs up
17AUG1945, 0818h	General Parker of Mukden Camp announced Armistice
19AUG1945, 1730h	Russians arrived, General Parker announced to POWs their liberation
27AUG1945	General Wainwright departed Mukden by air
29AUG1945	19-man Recovery Team #1 arrived at Mukden
11SEP1945	Departed by rail from Mukden to Port Arthur (Dalian), China
13SEP1945	USS Colbert departed Port Arthur for Okinawa
16SEP1945	Arrived in Okinawa, ordered back to sea due to Typhoon Ursula
16SEP1945	**#12 USS Colbert Struck by a Mine (During Typhoon Ursula)**
19SEP1945	William Frising (#1414) died from USS Colbert mine explosion.
~ 24SEP1945	Tug towed Colbert to Okinawa
27SEP1945	**#13 Flight to Manila in a B-24 Bombay**
01OCT1945	Journeyed home from Manila to Eunice LA via San Francisco and San Antonio
02FEB1946	Discharged in Hattiesburg MS

* Tottori Maru: Tabular Record of Movement
(combinedfleet.com/Tottori_t.htm)

Appendix C: Photo Credits

Photo 1: author's personal photo

Photo 2: author's personal photo

Photo 3: (1944) Dwight Eisenhower Speaks with Paratroopers [Photograph], Dwight D. Eisenhower Presidential Library

https:www.eisenhowerfoundation.net/sites/default/files/2021-05/D-Day_Eisenhower%20and%20the%20Troops_FINAL.pdf

Photo 4: Photo 4 Citation: n.d. (Alchetron, The Free Social Encyclopedia), [23JUL2023]

https://alchetron.com/Battle-of-Bataan#battle-of-bataan-0cef0fd6-f04d-4780-ad5c-b4c73d23b0c-resize-750.jpeg

Photo 5: (1942) Discussing Surrender Terms [Photograph], U.S. Army Center of Military History

https://history.army.mil/books/wwii/5-2/5-2_26.htm

Photo 6: (1942) Death March Starts [Photograph], Library of Congress

https://www.loc.gov/item/20011699980

Photo 7: author's personal photo

Photo 8: (n.d) Tottori Maru Hellship POW Carrier [Photograph], SEA Explorers Club [24JUL2023]

https://seaexplorersclub.com/totorri-maru-hellship/

Photo 9: (1944) USS Spearfish (SS-190) [Photograph] Naval History and Heritage Command htpps://www.history.navy.mil/content/history/nhhc/our-collections/photography/numerical-list-of-images/nhhc-series/naval-subjects-collection/l45--us-navy-ships/241-260/l45-267-03-01-uss-spearfish--ss-190-.html

Photo 10: James Bollich personal photo

Photo 11: James Bollich personal photo

Photo 12: (1942) General Wainwright broadcasting surrender instructions over Station KZRH, 07MAY1942 [Photograph], U.S. Army, Center of Military History,
https://history.army.mil/books/wwii/5-2/5-2_32.htm

Photo 13: (n.d) USS Colbert [Photograph], NavSource Online: Amphibious Photo Archive [24JUL2023] www.navsource.org/archives/10/03/03145.htm

Photo 14: (n.d) USS Colbert [Photograph], NavSource Online: Amphibious Photo Archive [24JUL2023] www.navsource.org/archives/10/03/03145.htm